THE SWORD
in Japanese
Martial Traditions

An Anthology of Articles from the Journal of Asian Martial Arts

Compiled by Michael A. DeMarco, M.A.

Disclaimer
Please note that the authors and publisher of this book are not responsible in any manner whatsoever for any injury that may result from practicing the techniques and/or following the instructions given within. Since the physical activities described herein may be too strenuous in nature for some readers to engage in safely, it is essential that a physician be consulted prior to training.

All Rights Reserved
No part of this publication, including illustrations, may be reproduced or utilized in any form or by any means, electronic or mechanical, including photocopying, recording, or by any information storage and retrieval system (beyond that copying permitted by sections 107 and 108 of the US Copyright Law and except by reviewers for the public press), without written permission from Via Media Publishing Company.

Warning: Any unauthorized act in relation to a copyright work may result in both a civil claim for damages and criminal prosecution.

Copyright © 2017
by Via Media Publishing Company

Articles in this anthology were originally published in the *Journal of Asian Martial Arts*, and from *Asian Marital Arts: Constructive Thoughts & Practical Applications* (2013) Listed according to the table of contents for this anthology:

Seckler, J. (1992), Vol. 1 No. 2, pp. 70-83
Taylor, K. (1993), Vol. 2 No. 3, pp. 36-63
Suino, N. (1994), Vol. 3 No. 3, pp. 84-91
Taylor, K. (1996), Vol. 5 No. 2, pp. 80-89
Taylor, K. (1997), Vol. 6 No. 1, pp. 80-103
Galas, M. (1997), Vol. 6 No. 3, pp. 20-47
Babin, M. (2000), Vol. 9 No. 4, pp. 36-51
Svinth, J. (2002), Vol. 11 No. 3, pp. 30-39
Suino, N. (2006), Vol. 15 No. 2, pp. 22-29
Bryant, A. (2009), Vol. 18 No. 4, pp. 64-71
Klens-Bigman, D. (2013), *Asian Marital Arts*, pp. 91-94
Taylor, K. (2013), *Asian Marital Arts*, pp. 133-136

Cover illustration
Magical artwork by Oscar Ratti, created directly from his feel for the Japanese fighting arts and a lifetime of academic research and budo practice.
© Futuro Designs and Publications

ISBN-13: 978-1893765481
ISBN-10: 1893765482

www.viamediapublishing.com

contents

preface

If the Way of the warrior is the soul of Japan, their magnificent swords were the tools utilized to form the nation and forge their spirit. You'll find an abundance of information in this special anthology in support of this thesis.

Kimberley Taylor wrote four chapters, the first being an interview with 7th-dan Matsuo Haruna. Haruna offers great advice for practitioners based on his first-hand experience. Taylor's two highly researched chapters give overviews of two major iaido schools. Excellent photos and descriptions of katas accompany the text. Taylor's finale is a short piece describing two of his favorite techniques, while Deborah Klens-Bigman's chapter deals with two of her favorite techniques.

Another top ranking swordsman, Nicklaus Suino, gets to the finicky details of sword-drawing techniques as performed by masters. From his two chapters, we learn how to watch for telltale signs of expertise and come to a greater appreciation of the art of drawing the sword.

Jonathan Seckler's chapter translates and comments on an essay written by Chozanshi Shissai in 1729. He argues that Neo-Confucianism rather than Zen became the foundation of swordsmanship, and illustrates how the sword arts began to be appreciated for their use for self-development.

Andrew Bryant's chapter focuses on poems passed down within the Muso Jiki-den Eishin-ryu School of Iaido. These poems correspond to techniques contained within the system created in the 17th century. The author presents each poem and offers provides textual descriptions of their corresponding applications with each sword technique illustrated.

Joseph Svinth's research presents the earliest kendo clubs to form in Canada. The socio-cultural settings add much flavor to this chapter. Information is provided regarding notable instructors, training, and competitions. Another way to better understand a martial tradition of one country is to compare it with another. Matthew Galas compares and contrasts sword arts in Germany with the Japanese traditions. The focus is on general principles and combat philosophy.

Devotees to sword practice are well award that scabbards get damaged. Michael Babin's chapter shows "how to" build a serviceable scabbard according talents of anyone moderately handy with tools.

The twelve chapters described above should inspire further research and practice in the Japanese sword arts, plus bring a greater appreciation for their unique place in world history and culture.

Michael A. DeMarco, Publisher
Santa Fe, New Mexico, December 2017

Swordsmanship and Neo-Confucianism: The Tengu's Art

Commentary and Translation by Jonathan Seckler, B.A.

Having no means of crossing this life,
I make swordsmanship my hiding place,
Sadly relying on it.

•

Good to make it a hiding place —
Swordsmanship has no use for fighting over things.[1]

These two *doka* by Yagyu Muneyoshi (1529-1606), the father of Yagyu Munenori, illustrate the attitudes of the samurai about swordsmanship in the Tokugawa period. Muneyoshi believed that swordsmanship need not be practical, an unusual idea prior to the seventeenth century. By the mid-eighteenth century, however, many samurai felt the same way. They began to view swordsmanship romantically, seeing it as a way to enlightenment and to enrich one's life, like practicing the tea ceremony, calligraphy, or studying Noh dance or chanting.

Hiroaki Sato notes that the *Fudochi Shinmyoroku*, a letter to Munenori from the Zen priest, Takuan (1573-1645), "was widely regarded as a bible by practitioners of the martial arts during the Tokugawa period."[2] The letter compares Zen to swordsmanship and claims that there are inexplicable links between the two.

Undeniably, many points of similarity can be found between Zen and swordsmanship. The same can be (and has been) said, however, of Zen and archery, Zen and the tea ceremony, and even Zen and writing! The fact is that Zen, with its emphasis on practice, concentration, and introspection, is compatible with an infinite number of activities. The link between Zen and swordsmanship is especially known in Japan, where many people are familiar with the saying, *kenzen ichi* (The sword and Zen are one). As G. Cameron Hurst points out, though, there is not necessarily a connection between the two. Indeed, few samurai warriors were believers in Zen.[3]

It is too simplistic to say that the purpose of swordsmanship was to teach Zen, as it provided a vehicle to teach Neo-Confucian ethics as well. During the Tokugawa period, military subjects were stressed as part of the traditional educational curriculum, to the extent that in some instances half the day was spent on drill and training. Swordsmanship in this case was used as part of the educational process. Zen, on the other hand, is anti-intellectual, downplaying the value of education.

Although swordsmanship is not connected only with Zen, it was a widespread belief as the popularity of the *Fudochi Shinmyoroku* indicates. To correct this, Chozanshi Shissai wrote the *Tengu Geijutsu Ron* (Essay on the Tengu's Art) in 1729. In it he argues that Zen is not the foundation of swordsmanship, but rather Neo-Confucianism is. Reinhard Kammer suggests that the work was fairly well known, appearing in various anthologies dealing with the philosophy of martial arts.[4] If so, then it seems that Shissai's contention, that Confucianism is at the heart of swordsmanship, must have been accepted by many swordsmen during the Tokugawa era. It is an oversight of Western scholars to focus only on the superficially analogous aspects of swordsmanship and Zen and ignore the existence of Neo-Confucianism. Therefore, Shissai's theories must be considered, as they illustrate some of the beliefs of the samurai regarding the uses and value of swordsmanship in Tokugawa Japan.

Chozanshi Shissai (1659-1741)

Not much is known about this writer. In the introduction to the *Tengu Geijutsu Ron*, the editor notes that he was active during the Kyoho era (1716-1735) in Osaka.[5] He was a Daoist as well as a Confucian and Zen scholar. Besides the *Tengu Geijutsu Ron*, he wrote such works as a satire entitled *Inaka soshi* (The Provincial Zhuang-zi) and a "moral work," the *Ikkyu mondo* (A Dialogue with Ikkyu). The *Tengu Geijutsu Ron* is not his only treatise on martial arts. Before completing it, he also wrote a humorous essay entitled,

Neko no Myojutsu (The Wondrous Art of the Cat), in which he interviews a cat that has succeeded in catching a particularly large rat.

It is interesting that Shissai was not a famous swordsman himself. In the *Tengu Geijutsu Ron* he states that his goal was to apply the principles of Confucianism not only to swordsmanship, where they are inherent, he claimed, but to other aspects of life as well.

The *Tengu Geijutsu Ron*

The *Tengu Geijutsu Ron* is an essay in four parts that discusses the philosophical ideas behind the art of swordsmanship. It was meant to be read only by practitioners of swordsmanship. As a result, it contains a great many technical and sometimes esoteric terms. It is organized as a dialogue between Shissai, a questioner, and a *tengu*, the respondent, a mythical creature reputed to be a master of swordsmanship. The famous hero of the *Heike Monogatari*, Minamoto Yoshitsune, so legend has it, was taught the arts of swordsmanship and strategy from a tengu on Mt. Kurama.

Shissai never discusses the technical aspects of swordsmanship, referring to them always as *gokusoku* or *gokui*, the secret essence or mystery of the art. Shissai's major concerns are the ideas and results of the practice of swordsmanship rather than the technical aspects. Yoshida Yutaka has condensed the major tenants of Shissai into twelve main points in his collection, *Budo Hiden Sho* (Martial Arts' Secret Writings).[6] I have translated his edition here. Yoshida has added titles to his excerpts which I have sometimes condensed or changed as I saw fit. After many excerpts, I have elaborated on the main points to emphasize how Japanese swordsmanship was influenced both by Zen and Neo-Confucian ideas.

FIRST, ONE SHOULD UNIFY THE MIND AND BODY

When one gains fullness in his learning, one's mind and body are unified as the principle contained in his learning becomes clear by itself. When his understanding becomes deep enough and all uncertainty is gone, principles (*ri*) and techniques will be totally united, resulting in the calming of the mental force (*ki*) and the complete stabilization of the spirit. Then one's movements will become fluid and free. Since ancient times, this has been the process of learning any of the arts.[7] Therefore, practice is essential for the arts. If one's skill is not fully developed, one's mental force will not be contained; if one's mental force is not contained, then the mind and body will not be natural.

The mind and body become two separate entities and their free fusion will not be accomplished.

Comment

In this first section, Shissai is declaring unequivocally the precedence of Neo-Confucianism within swordsmanship. By explicitly using the two terms *ri* and *ki* to denote universal principles and mental or spiritual force, he says that the practice of swordsmanship will aid one to become an enlightened human or, in the terminology of the Confucians, a sage. I have translated *ri* as "principle." He uses *ki* to refer to mental and spiritual energy, so I have translated this term as "mental force." The belief that techniques and principle are the two integral parts of swordsmanship is a distinctly Neo-Confucian idea. These two components are the equivalent of the Neo-Confucian components of the universe, *ki* and *ri*. The Neo-Confucian belief is that the universe in its entirety is composed of various combinations of mental force and principle. By making this point early in his essay, Shissai implies that the principles of swordsmanship are not based on Zen. This is in direct contrast with some modern scholars who believe that Zen and swordsmanship were intricately linked together.[8]

Shissai's observation that, if techniques and principle are not unified, then the mind and body will be separate, is also similar to Yagyu Munenori's belief that being conscious of one's actions is detrimental. In the *Heiho Kadensho*, he states, "If you are conscious of shooting an arrow . . . you will not be able to take aim properly. If you are conscious of using a sword . . . you will not be able to hold steady the tip of the word."[9]

LAMENTING THE TEMPERAMENT OF TODAY'S PRACTITIONER

In the past, those intent [on learning martial arts] were rich with passion and firm in determination. In their pursuit of mastery, they were industrious, were never defeated, and were never idle. They obeyed the teacher's instructions unquestionably. Day and night they practiced, testing what they had been taught. If they had doubts, they asked their comrades. Thus, as their skills matured, they themselves understood the ultimate principles [of the universe]. Therefore, their comprehension pierced deep into their beings. The master taught the fundamental techniques; he did not speak of the principles contained in them. He just waited for his students to come to understand on their own.

4

This is known as "drawing [the bow], but not releasing [the arrow]."[10] It is not that the teacher did not speak because he was stingy. At that stage of learning, the master just wanted his students to think for themselves and to perfect their practice.

As Confucius said, "If I draw one corner, and he cannot transfer it to the three others, I do not repeat it."[11] This is the ancients' way of teaching. As a result, [students in] both scholarship and the arts are full of sincerity and rich in skill.

Nowadays, however, human emotions are poor and the will is not intense enough. From youth, people avoid toil and prefer what's easy; they desire to develop their skills swiftly by mastering superficially clever "tricks." If these young people were taught the old ways, there would not be any more students! These days the teacher has to show them the way of swordsmanship, and he has to instruct even beginners with the most secret techniques. He has to show how they work; moreover, the teacher has to lead them by the hand! Even so, there are many who become disinterested and quit.

Such people who do continue training develop their grasp of the principles haughtily, not being satisfied with the ways of the ancients. Although their practice is weak, they expect their skills to become good enough to reach the heavens. This is how time is forcing the situation to be shaped.

Comment

In this section, Shissai depicts the current practice of swordsmanship as having deteriorated greatly. The major points Shissai makes are that practice is important, that samurai should be following the ancient ways, and that they are not training correctly.

The importance of practice is almost self-explanatory. As Shissai says, if one does not practice then one will not understand the essence of the techniques completely. As Miyamoto Musashi, the famous swordsman, writes, "Practicing a thousand days is said to be discipline, practicing ten thousand days is said to be refining. This should be carefully studied."[12]

How a samurai practices is also very important. Shissai says that the ancient's way of teaching is the correct path to follow. By "ancient's way," he means following Confucian ideals, quoting from *Confucian Analects*. Shissai is implying that Confucianism is at the heart of swordsmanship. In contrast, Musashi says that the paths of Confucius and Buddha are not correct paths for the warrior.

The idea that swordsmen in the mid-Tokugawa era were not training

5

earnestly enough is a common theme in many texts on martial arts. Both Daidoji Yuzan, in the *Budo Shoshinshu*, and Yamamoto Tsunetomo, in *Hagakure*, also take up this topic in great detail.[13] Both of these writers were considered reactionary during the time, and ultraconservative.[14] Nevertheless, this was a common theme during the Tokugawa era and it shows to what extent the practice of swordsmanship had declined.

CAN A SUPERIOR PRIEST BE A SKILLED SWORDSMAN?

I asked: Can Zen monks who have transcended life and death perform swordsmanship freely?

The Tengu answers: The purpose of Zen monks' practice is different [from a martial artist's]. The Zen monk dislikes the cycle of life and death and hopes to enter nirvana, so from the beginning he is one who has placed himself in fatal situations in order to transcend life and death. Therefore, once he is surrounded by many enemies and his body may be cut to bits, he can easily maintain a calm spirit. But this is not for the purpose of living. Rather, he is simply not afraid of dying.

Comment

Shissai contends here that, while Zen does offer potential benefits, there is a major difference between the Zen monk and the swordsman. Zen monks train themselves in order to become enlightened; they wish to transcend this world which they consider to be only ephemeral and transient. To do this, they train in order to lose their fear of death.

Swordsmen however, train for a different reason. They train in order to participate in life and to serve in society as its rulers. Therefore, they must inculcate themselves with the values of the ruling class, which in Tokugawa Japan are Neo-Confucian in nature.

THE FUTILITY OF A BEGINNER LEARNING FROM ZEN MONKS

I ask: What about frequently referred to cases of swordsmen of old who have met a Zen monk and learned the secrets of swordsmanship?

The Tengu answers: Zen monks do not teach the secrets of swordsmanship. It's just that when your spirit is calm, you can respond to situations properly. When you loathe to part with life, that attachment to life becomes a cause for pain. When you are troubled and your spirit is in utter chaos, you do nothing but imperil your own life.

The swordsman in question has worked for many years at his art, never fully resting, training his mental force, and drilling in technique. But to such a person, the essence of swordsmanship will remain closed to him even after he has fought many duels.

He spent many years in vain pursuit of mastery, but upon meeting with a Zen monk, he realizes the meaning of life and death on his own, and upon hearing that the myriad things are only the reflections of one's mind, his own troubled mind is instantly freed and his spirit is calmed. Consequently, he is freed from the worries of this world and is able to practice swordsmanship freely.

I am referring to those who have spent a long time struggling spiritually, practicing the techniques, and finally succeeding in freeing themselves from the maze they were caught in. It does not happen all at once. It is the same as saying that one gained enlightenment by receiving a blow from the stick of a superior Zen master. It is not something that can be rushed. An inexperienced seeker in an art who meets with a learned priest and is given an opportunity to hear his wisdom will not gain enlightenment.

Comment

While Shissai does admit that there is some value in learning from a Zen master, he qualifies it by saying that only those who have already worked for a long time swordsmanship will benefit. Zen in this instance is merely an opening discovered that bring swordsmanship to a higher plateau after years of seeking. Yet it is interesting Shissai does value the contributions that Zen can make to swordsmanship when only a spiritual breakthrough can help a swordsman to advance his skill.

LET DISCIPLINE OF TECHNIQUES AND THE SPIRIT BE ONE AND THE SAME

As a rule, one who is proficient in one art, because he constantly trains his spirit, understands the principle of any and everything. But the intent of such men is focused primarily on their own art. Hence they fail to grasp the principles of the universe.

Even though there are people who enjoy scholarship, they make art the master and the study of the Way a guest, and as a result, the deep principles that are learned are all made to be the servants of the arts. Thus, such people do not become useful to other matters.

So how does one promote the training of the spirit? If one who trains in the arts comes to understand the relationship of principles and arts, then daily practice in the arts will benefit one's spirit. The evidence of this understanding is the fact that one will have mastered the Way of nature. At this point, one's art has become completely free.

But there are those who, from the beginning, become overly attached to a single way and cannot free themselves from it. If in both scholarship and in the arts, one can abandon this narrow-mindedness, then one cannot be moved by any outside forces in this world, and then one will be able to respond to any needs, free of obstructions and attachments.

This sense of attachment is not just limited to things like gold, silver, property, passions, desires, or pretensions. Even if one is not evil, if one is even slightly attached to one thought, then that is none other than attachment. If it is a light attachment, it will block the union of mind and body a little bit; if it is an intense attachment, then the union of mind and body will be blocked a great deal.

One who is proficient in art is expected to know clearly that an attachment will cause him harm. But it is not something he will understand among the wide uses of the mind and body. Even while one is trained in the matters of the spirit, one cannot easily learn about the principles of the universe nor see something which can only be discovered with great concentration.

It is I who train for the spiritual aspect, and it is also I who work in the arts. There are not two separate minds in this pursuit. This point one should give careful thought.

Comment

In this section, Shissai again declares that practice is most important if one is to excel in swordsmanship. However he also suggests that swordsmanship and literary scholarship are not incompatible. The stress on academic study is Confucian in nature, as a Zen monk would never suggest scholarship as a means to attain enlightenment. This idea is further borne out in Munenori's oft-quoted text, the *Heiho Kadensho*, where he says that the way to begin to achieve the Way (meaning, in this case, perfection with the sword) is to study (both literary and military arts) diligently. It is important to realize that Munenori, although much influenced by Zen, accepts the value of learning as part of swordsmanship. Morigawa Tetsuro repeats Shissai's idea that the practice of all arts offers the same potential benefits, writing that "whether art or scholarship—all Ways are the same."[15]

Also in the first paragraph of the section above, Shissai attacks narrow-mindedness in practicing swordsmanship and other traditional arts. He is criticizing people who practice swordsmanship so intensely that, although they may come to understand the broader applications the arts have, they do not apply them in their lives. As a result, Shissai says that these people are limited. This is related to the Neo-Confucian value of practicality. Leaders and scholars should be conversant in a variety of disciplines; specialization is to be avoided. A swordsman who knew nothing but swordsmanship would be a poor leader of men. And swordsmanship is supposed to promote leadership, transmitting as it does the values and beliefs of the samurai.

Shissai also spends some time on the concept of attachment. Here it is used in the Confucian sense of the term. To the Confucians, an evil person is one who seeks to gain profit for himself. Hence the terms for being attached to things and evil are similar to the Confucian. Shissai bears this out when he discusses attachment to worldly possessions as not just limited to things like gold, silver, etc. Shissai claims that occupation with oneself hinders the practice of the arts, a Neo-Confucian rather than a Zen idea, as Zen can be described as being somewhat selfish in nature, since it requires total dedication and concentration on oneself.

THERE IS A GREAT DANGER IN THE PREMATURE ENLIGHTENMENT OF BEGINNERS

I ask: I have many children who are still young. How should I train them in swordsmanship?

The Tengu answers: As for young people who do not have the [intellectual] strength to understand the principles of the universe, withhold any discussion on trivial matters. Instead, for the time being, they must obey the master absolutely, learn suitable techniques and practice their hand- and foot-work, making their bodies strong. On top of this they should discipline their mental force and train their minds. Meanwhile, they may come close to discovering the mysteries [of the art by themselves].[16] This is the order of training. . . .

If, from the beginning of training, without developed techniques, [children] should say, "I will empty my mind to let the techniques develop naturally and let gentleness control strength. Learning the techniques is the last concern of mine," then they will become stubborn and lazy and they will not have a [good] foundation, becoming dropouts now as well as in later life.

Comment

Children of the samurai were introduced to swordsmanship at a young age. Here Shissai offers his views on how to best train children in swordsmanship. He suggests that they be trained under a master who will first teach them the fundamentals of swordsmanship and develop their bodies and not confuse them with especially difficult techniques. Training of the mind comes later, but, like adults, they are encouraged to discover the inner meaning of swordsmanship for themselves. I have waited until the end of the next two sections to comment on them.

IN THE TRUE NATURE OF MAN, THE MIND IS CALM

I ask: What is something that is "moving, but not moving; still, but not still?"

The Tengu answers: Humans are living beings. They cannot remain still. There are many daily matters and many duties to attend to, but the mind that does not move for things and that remains free of desires and selfishness is firmly settled and completely in control.

Speaking in terms of swordsmanship, though you may be surrounded by many enemies and fighting to the right and left, you must transcend life-and-death and become tranquil. Despite these many enemies, your mind should not sway; this is the meaning of "moving, but not moving."

Haven't you seen someone ride a horse? A good rider, though the horse gallops to the east or to the west, is calm and unhurried, and his body is peaceful and unmoving.

Viewed from our vantage point, the horse and rider seem to be united. However, the rider only controls the animal; he does not fight against its nature. So one could say that the rider sits astride the saddle and is master of the horse. But the horse does not seem bothered by this and carries on contentedly. The horse forgets the man; the man forgets the horse. Their spirits are united and inseparable. This could be described as "there is no man above the saddle, and no horse below the saddle." This is an example of "moving, but not moving," as it is easy to see.

[In contrast,] a beginner will attempt to control the horse against its nature; thus he himself will not be at peace. Because he and the horse are separate and struggle for different ends, when the horse runs, its entire body will move and it will grow weary.

From a book about horsemanship, here is a poem cited as written by a horse:

I try to gallop with full force,
But I am pulled back. Being pulled by the
Mouth, I cannot go, though I want to.[17]

This is an attempt, in the place of a horse, to express how the horse must feel. This is not just about horses, this [kind of] spirit should not be used when having men work for you. When you place trivial reasons ahead of the nature of all things, you will become agitated and the cause of suffering to others.

ALTHOUGH I SAY BE STILL, DON'T NEGLECT THE VALUE OF MOVEMENT

What do I mean by "still, but not still"? When the feelings of joy and anger are not allowed to develop, then nothing is hoarded in the mind and body as vanity." From this comes stillness and the cessation of the passions so that the body will obey, respond freely, and not be attached to outside distractions. Being still and unmoving is the heart's actual state; the ability to respond to change is the heart's purpose. Its state is being still, comprehending the various principles, a clear spirit. Its purpose is to obey the commands of heaven and to respond to these principles. Both state and use come from one source. This is what is meant by "moving, but not moving; still, but not still."

When speaking of swordsmanship, it lies in taking up arms against the enemy. Being impartial, you should not hate, nor should you fear. In the midst of battle, you should not plan this or that, nor should you have any thoughts. Then, when the enemy attacks, your mind and body will obey and your reactions will be unhindered and free.

Although your body moves, you will not lose the state of stillness; although your heart is still, do not neglect the use of movement. In a mirror's face there is nothing, but the entire universe is reflected in it; although shapes appear, when they leave, their reflections do not remain. The image of the moon on the water is the same. The clarity of the mind and body is also just so. When an inferior person moves, in this movement he loses himself; when he is still, he becomes stubborn and cannot respond to the world.

Comment

This idea, of a peaceful, unmoving spirit can be found in the writings of various Zen practitioners. It is ironic that Shissai, who seemed to feel that Zen had little to contribute to swordsmanship, should discuss this at length. This

11

concept is called *ku* (emptiness) by both Musashi and Munenori. Musashi considered this idea so important that he devoted one whole section to it in the *Go Rin No Sho* [The Book of Five Rings]. He defines *ku* as being "that which cannot be known."[19] By practicing martial arts until one understands and sees to the heart of all things, Musashi says emptiness is attained.

Munenori's view is very similar. True emptiness is the state of the mind. The mind is nothingness, yet it is the master of the body. Enlightenment comes from recognizing this.

Shissai's view is the same as Munenori's. The mind should be empty and peaceful. When it is, then one's body moves quickly and effortlessly. Just like the example of a horse and rider, when the mind is peaceful, then movement is natural. When movement is natural, separation between the mind and the body cannot be discerned, like the link between horse and rider.

THE METAPHOR OF THE MOVING MIND: SUIGETSU

I ask: What is *"Suigetsu"* [the moon in the water]?

The Tengu answers: Although different schools attach various meanings to this metaphor, virtually all use it to reflect the spontaneity of nature as the moon and the water combine, as illustrated in an emperor's[20] poem about a hermit's cave at the pond of Hirosawa:

> Being reflected, the moon does not think;
> Reflecting, the water, too does not think —
> Hirosawa's Pond.[21]

In the heart of this imperial poem is an explanation of the spontaneity of nature. Again, in the heavens, there is one moon, but every stream seems to contain it. It is not that the light is divided up in the waters that reflect it. For if there is not water, there is no reflection. Also, the moon's shadow does not come from within the water itself. Whether it is reflected in all streams or in just one stream, to the moon it does not matter. Nor does the size of the [body of] water make a difference. By means of this metaphor, you can understand the wondrous effect of the combination of mind and body. This is all I will speak of concerning the good and bad of water.

But the moon has form and color; the spirit does not. Something that is easy to see, having form and color, is used to illustrate something that does not. Such is the case with everything. So do not take this story literally!

12

Comment

This excerpt, as well as the next two, is a description of esoteric terms used by many schools of martial arts to describe various mental states and feelings. The use of the metaphor of the moon on the water is common to many different schools of martial arts. Yoshida mentions that the metaphor was first used by Munenori.[22] It is also used extensively by the Hozoin-ryu of spearmanship. In the Hozoin-ryu, the metaphor is used to describe the importance of knowing one's opponent's actions so that one can protect oneself.

Similarly, Munenori described the metaphor in terms of *ma*, or "space." One judges the distance between oneself and one's opponent so as to know where one's safety zone is, like the moon on the water, which casts only its shadow or reflection on the water, never coming into contact with the water itself.

In contrast to Munenori, Shissai uses the metaphor to illustrate the spontaneity of nature. Like water reflecting the moon, which does not seek to project itself on the water, nature does not seek to act; it just exists.

NOT LOSING ONE'S ORIGINAL NATURE

I ask: In many schools there is something called "*zanshin*." I do not understand it; what is *zanshin*?

The Tengu answers: *Zanshin* is not a technique of enlightenment; it only means that the original state of the mind and body is unmoving. When the mind and body are unmoving, reactions are clear. It is the same in daily life.

Even if you were to plunge into the depths of hell swinging your swords, your self is your basic self.[23] Therefore, you can act freely and without restraint, guarding the front and back, the left and the right. It is not that one part of your heart enters the movement and one part remains. When your spirit remains, there are two thoughts. And if your mind and body are not clear while your spirit tries to enter [the movement], then you will strike and thrust about blindly. Clarity comes from a stable mind and body. Then [with an unmoving mind and body] one can strike and thrust cleanly. This is difficult to understand, and if you misunderstand, then you are in danger of hurting yourself.

Comment

The term *zanshin* is very similar to the concept of *ku*. It refers to the nature of an unmoving heart that allows one to act instantly. The term is also used by the Tenshin Shoden Katori Shinto-ryu to describe the state of mind of an attacker whose entire concentration is in his movement. All movements should ideally be made in a state of *zanshin*.

THE CONCEPT OF INITIATIVE

In many schools, there is an idea known as *initiative*. This is a term used for the beginner to help him promote courage and discourage laziness. Actually, with an unmoving mind and body, you will not lose your self. When your body is filled with a generous mental force, you will always have the initiative.

It is not the purpose of the spirit to strike first. But in virtually all of swordsmanship, it is necessary to foster a lively mental force and avoid a sluggish one. Whether waiting in the midst of attack or attacking in the midst of waiting, both are natural reactions. Only for the beginner have temporary names been temporarily attached [to these concepts]. The saying, "moving, but not moving; still, but not still" is the heart of it.

You should not limit the beginner by not discussing strong and weak *ki*. Therefore, such things have been given a name to teach beginners. But when one attaches a name to something, being obsessed with the name is to miss the larger meaning. If you do not attach a name to things, then there is no meaning and you cannot recognize things. He who does not understand the meanings of "rabbit" and "horn" will not understand such things when they are explained to them.[24] Such is the case with all things. So people learn from teachers, and if there is no one who can teach, then concealing [the secrets of swordsmanship] is also acceptable. That way, people will discover the greater meaning of swordsmanship by themselves—through observation and examination.

Comment

Here, Shissai is emphasizing the importance of developing a strong and positive attitude in the practice of martial arts, especially in regard to taking the initiative. The connection between one's attitude and one's skill in anything is much more extensive than is obvious. Shissai here is emphasizing this connection, exhorting swordsmen to be vigorous in practice. The result Shissai promises is that then one will always have the initiative.

THE SECRET OF SWORDSMANSHIP

I ask: Swordsmanship has a wondrous effect on the mind and body. Why is it kept secret?

The Tengu answers: The principle of swordsmanship is the principle of the universe. If I can understand this, then anyone should be able to. One keeps it secret for the beginner. If it was not mysterious, the beginner would not believe it. This is simply an expedient teaching method. Therefore, the end of all teachings is secret. Yet, there is no mystery. The beginner does not discern between things; he listens without reason and discriminates poorly by himself. Consequently, when he talks to others, he can cause great harm. Therefore, he is not taught all, but only the things he can understand. Once someone understands the secrets [of swordsmanship], however, even if he is not from the same school as you, you should not conceal the wider lessons from him.

Comment

Finally, Shissai addresses the importance of keeping certain teaching secret. Beginning swordsmen often do not understand the lessons of their teachers fully and, when they begin to discuss them, mislead others. That is the only reason for keeping the principles of swordsmanship secret. Once one has reached a full understanding of the arts, one should teach them to everyone.

The *Tengu Geijutsu Ron* illustrates the influences that Neo-Confucianism and Zen had on swordsmanship during the Tokugawa period. Written for the purpose of extending the principles and ideas of swordsmanship beyond the art itself, it attacks the idea that swordsmanship and Zen are linked, at the same time that it uses some of the same ideas that are found in Zen. The two main conclusions that Shissai makes are that swordsmanship should be used to transmit Confucianism and that the link to Zen is not as strong as it is popularly believed.

Shissai makes his beliefs about Confucianism obvious from the very beginning when he discusses the importance of unifying the mind and body by unifying *ki* and *ri*. The importance of *ri* is repeated throughout the text. The highest principle inherent in nature according to the Neo-Confucianists is that humans must strive to become well-educated and moral beings, so as to participate in society. Shissai claims that this principle is the same one underlying swordsmanship. Furthermore, his exhortations to practice and to obey the teacher absolutely are also Confucian beliefs about teaching.

Shissai's second conclusion, that the connection between Zen and swordsmanship is erroneous, is also obvious. He states very plainly that students who seek instruction from Zen priests do not benefit by it without long years of training beforehand. The reason that studying with a Zen priest is not as beneficial as might be believed is due to the overall purpose of Zen. The purpose of the Zen priest is to train for death so that he may transcend life. The purpose of the swordsman, on the other hand, should be to train for life so that he may participate in society as a member of the ruling class.

While Shissai does claim that Zen has no place in swordsmanship, it is ironic that he mentions some concepts that are similar to Zen. The most notable of these is the importance that he places on the saying, "moving, but not moving; still, but not still." It is remarkably similar to the Yagyu Shinkage-ryu and the Niten Ichi-ryu's concepts of *ku*, or "emptiness." The importance that he places on the mind or heart in this instance is also common in Zen.

Another Zen-like concept that Shissai mentions is the metaphor of *suigetsu*, or of the moon on the water. Again the Yagyu Shinkage-ryu uses this metaphor extensively, as does the Hozoin-ryu of spearmanship, another Zen inspired school of martial arts.

Shissai's borrowing of these Zen concepts for his essay on swordsmanship might be taken as hypocritical, given this criticism of Zen. But when looking at what the samurai thought about swordsmanship in the Tokugawa period, one finds that Zen and Confucianism, were often combined to form a complete philosophical system. Zen allowed the swordsman to perfect his spiritual side and his physical techniques; Confucianism on the other hand, trained the warrior for participation in society. Both together combined into the tengu's art; after all, the tengu does not care what influences swordsmanship.

Note

1 Quoted in Inamura Yoshio. (1967). *Shiryo Yagyu Shinkage-ryu* [Historical materials of the Yagyu Shinkage-ryu]. Tokyo: Shin Jinbutsu Orai Sha. Translation by Hiroaki Sato. (1985). *The Sword and the Mind*. Woodstock, NY: The Overlook Press, p. 15.

2 Sato, p. 17.

3 G. Cameron Hurst III. (in press). *The Martial Arts of Japan*. New Haven: Yale University Press, p. 283.

4 Reinhard Kammer. (1978). *The Art of the Sword: The Tengu geijutsu ron of Chozan Shissai*. (Betty Fitzgerald, trans.). Boston: Arkana, p. 12.

[5] Shissai Chozanshi. (1957). *Tengo Geijutsu Ron, in Nihon Tetsugaku shiso zensho* [Complete collection of Japanese philosophical thought], Vol. 15. (Saigusa Hiroto and Miyagawa Akira, Eds.). Tokyo: Heibonsha, p. 205.

[6] Yutaka Yoshida. (1968). *Budo Hidensho*. Tokyo: Tokuma Shoten, pp. 213-236.

[7] Although Yoshida only refers to martial arts in his translation, in my view Shissai is implying that in all arts this is so, not just swordsmanship.

[8] See, for example, Thomas Cleary, *The Japanese Art of War* (1991). Boston: Shambhala and Hiroaki Sato, *The Sword and the Mind*.

[9] Sato, p. 74.

[10] This phrase is written in Chinese, as opposed to the rest of the text; evidently it is an allusion to a Chinese source. Yoshida paraphrases this as "bringing one close [to observe], but not explaining it," p. 218. The idea is to expose younger students to the techniques while allowing them to discover the inner meaning themselves.

[11] Yoshida edited this quotation from his selection; it is from Confucius, *Analects*, VII: 8. In the *Analects of Confucius*, translated by Arthur Waley (New York: Vintage Books, 1938), p. 124, the complete version of this saying is as follows:

> The Master said, "Only one who bursts with eagerness do I instruct; only one who bubbles with excitement, do I enlighten. If I hold up one corner and a man cannot come back to me with the other three, I do not continue the lesson."

Again, the interpretation is that Confucius did not openly show his students everything; he showed them the basics and waited for them to understand by their own efforts.

[12] Minyamoto Musashi. (1982). *The Book of Five Rings* (Translated with commentary by Bradford Brown, Y. Kashiwagi, W. Barrett, and E. Sasagawa). New York: Bantam Books, p. 53.

[13] Daidoji Yuzan's text has been translated by A.K. Sadler as *The Code of the Samurai* (Rutland, VT: Charles A. Tuttle Company, 1941) and Yamamoto Tsunetomo's work has been translated by William Scott Wilson (New York: Kodansha International, Ltd., 1979).

[14] Hurst. (1990). "Death, Honor and Loyalty: The Bushido Ideal," *Philosophy East and West*, 40(4): 511-527, p. 514.

[15] Morigawa, Tetsuro. (n.d.). *Nihon Bushidoshi* [The History of Japanese Bushido]. Tokyo: Nihon Bungeisha, p. 108.

[16] In my view, this is similar to Shissai's statement earlier that the teacher shows only the basic techniques.

[17] Translated by Andrew T. Tsubaki. Kammer translates this poem as follows (p. 68):

> At first he whips me,
> But should I care to go,
> He restrains me
> And holds fast to the reins
> So that I cannot take a step.

[18] This sentence alludes to the *Chung yung* (Doctrine of the Mean), a Neo-Confucian text, which reads, "When the passions of joy, anger, grief, and delight are not manifested then they are said to be *chung* [in due medium]."

[19] Musashi, p. 106.

[20] Emperor Sutoku (r. 1123-1141).

[21] Kammer's translation (p. 69):

> The moon casts its reflection unwittingly
> Upon waters which have no desire to hold it
> In the Pond of Hirosawa.

Kammer notes that the Pond of Hirosawa was a popular place for moon viewing, located in the Saga district of Kyoto.

[22] Yoshida, p. 23 1.

[23] i.e., one's original nature is not lost. Yoshida, p. 232.

[24] They must be experienced directly.

References

Cleary, Thomas. (199 1). *The Japanese Art of War: Learning the Culture of Strategy*. Boston: Shambala Publications.

Hurst, G. Cameron III. (1990). Death, honor and loyalty: The bushido ideal. *Philosophy East and West* 40(4), 511-527 (forthcoming). *The Martial Arts of Japan, Volume One: Swordsmanship and Archery*. New Haven: Yale University Press.

Inamura, Yoshio. (1967). *Shiryo Yagyu Shinkage-ryu*. [Historical materials of the Yagyu Shinkage-ryu]. Tokyo: Shin Jinbutsu Orai Sha.

Kammer, Reinhard. (1978). *The Art of the Sword: The Tengu geijutsu ron of Chozan Shissai*. (Betty Fitzgerald, Trans.). Boston: Arkana.

Miyamoto, Musashi. (1982). *The Book of Five Rings.* (Translated with commentary by Bradford Brown, Y. Kashiwagi, W. Barrett, and E. Sasagawa). New York: Bantam Books.

Morigawa, Tetsuro. (n.d.). *Nihon Bushidoshi.* [History of Japanese bushido]. Tokyo: Nihon Geijutsu Shoten.

Reid, Howard and Croucher, Michael. (1983). *The Way of the Warrior.* New York: Simon and Schuster.

Sadler, A.K. (1941). *The Code of the Samurai.* Rutland, VT: Charles A. Tuttle Company.

Sato, Hiroaki (Translator). (1985). *The Sword and the Mind.* Woodstock, NY: The Overlook Press.

Shissai, Chozanshi. (1957). Tengu geijutsu ron [Essay on the Tengu's art]. In *Nihon tetsugaku shiso zensho* [Complete collection of Japanese philosophical thought] (Vol. 15). (Saigusa Hiroto and Miyagawa Akira, Eds.). Tokyo: Heibonsha.

Takuan. (1984). *The Unfettered Mind.* (William Scott Wilson, Trans.). New York: Kodansha International, Ltd.

Waley, Arthur. (1938). *The Analects of Confucius.* New York: Vintage Books.

Yamamoto, Tsunetomo. (1979). *Hagakure.* (William Scott Wilson, Trans.). New York: Kodansha International, Ltd.

Yoshida, Yutaka. (1968). *Budo hidensho.* [Martial arts' secret writings] Tokyo: Tokuma Shoten.

The History of Iaido: A Japanese Sword Art
by Kimberley Taylor, M.Sc.

Matsuo Haruna, 7th dan Kyoshi from Ohara, Okuyama, Japan;
1989 All Japan Champion; Executing *waki-no-kamai* in inset.
Photos courtesy of K. Taylor, except where noted.

Introduction

The Japanese sword art of iaido is described in this chapter and examples of *kata* (fundamental forms, techniques or movements) from several levels of practice are given. These levels correspond roughly to historical periods in the Muso Jikiden Eishin-ryu, one of the major iaido *ryu* (schools). A lineage of the *soke*[1] (headmaster) of the Muso Jikiden Eishin-ryu and a genealogy of related schools is also provided.

At the beginning of the seventeenth century several events favored the development of iaido and other *budo* (martial Ways). Most importantly, the country was unified militarily by Saito Dosan, Oda Nobunaga, Toyotomi Hideyoshi and finally Tokugawa Ieyasu, who established the Tokugawa Shogunate. It was Hideyoshi who first established the status of the populace, the *daimyo* (lords), samurai, farmers, artisans and merchants. Hideyoshi denied commoners the *katana* or long sword, reserving this privilege for the daimyo and samurai.

These developments entrenched Japan in a modified feudal system which was to last for well over two hundred years until the Emperor Meiji regained political power for the Imperial house. Two centuries of peace, prosperity and social stasis provided the ruling samurai class the leisure time to codify *bujutsu*[2] (martial arts) into schools which became *budo*. Today the phrase "Japanese martial arts" usually refers to *budo* which were developed from 1600 to about 1860 and the more modern arts derived from these.

When the Tokugawa Era began, mounted warriors were no longer needed, and many samurai were cast loose to become "wave men," or *ronin*, who wandered about the countryside looking for work or turning to banditry. Since only the landed classes could still afford horses, most warriors now went about on foot. It was partly in response to this fact that the "new sword," or *shin-to*, became popular. This sword was usually shorter and heavier than the *tachi* and was mounted so that it could be placed through the belt-edge up, to allow it to be drawn horizontally or sky-to-ground instead of the more usual ground-to-sky draw of the *tachi*. The *tachi* draw was designed so that the sword would clear a horse's head. The *katana* or *shin-to* draw was designed to clear the scabbard quickly so that the sword was in attacking position immediately.

With thousands of unemployed warriors wandering the countryside and few wars to fight, the style of swordsmanship changed. Instead of armored enemies facing each other in groups with swords drawn, the surprise attack and small fight became common and the art of the quick draw was developed. *Kenjutsu* was the term used to describe fighting with swords already drawn, and *iaijutsu*, the simultaneous draw and cut. With no armor to hack through, one-handed cuts from the draw became practical as did vertical cuts to the head since there was no helmet to interfere.

A few accomplished warriors began to realize that, through years of effort and devotion to sword practice, they had arrived at an understanding of their own nature. Because of these men, the *bujutsu* represented by *satsujin-no-ken* (the sword that takes life) became the *budo* represented by *katsujin-no-ken* (the sword that gives life). The intention of the student of *bujutsu* was to learn how to defeat an opponent, while the intention of the student of *budo* was to learn to defeat one's own ego.

The man generally credited with the origination of iaido is Jinsuke Shigenobu (Hayashizuki), who lived through the Momoyama Period when the three unifiers, Oda, Hideyoshi and Ieyasu conquered Japan. The art he founded between 1601 and 1615 is usually termed *Shinmei Muso-ryu Batto Jutsu*. He was later given the title of first headmaster of the Muso Jikiden Eishin-ryu. From his teachings several hundred schools of iai were developed, of which some twenty to thirty are still extant. A listing of some of these schools and their relationship is given later.

The seventh headmaster of the Muso Jikiden line was a man named Hasegawa Chikaranosuke Eishin, who added to the school a set of *tatehiza* (raised knee) techniques usually called Eishin-ryu. Prior to this time, the school included techniques executed from both *tatehiza* and a standing position.

Omori Rokurozaemon Masamitsu was a student said to have been expelled from the school by Eishin at one time. Omori was a student of *Ogasawara Buke Reiho*, or etiquette, as well as the Shinkage school of sword. The Shinkage-ryu had a set of five iai techniques called the *Saya-no-uchi Batto Gohan*. Rokurozaemon developed a set of techniques, later called the Omori-ryu, which were initiated from the formal seated posture called *seiza*. For this innovation (and probably an apology) Eishin re-admitted him to the school.

In the Taisho Era (1912-1926), the seventeenth headmaster, Oe Masamichi (Shikei) (1852-1927), incorporated the Omori waza as the introductory level. Shikei is the man who named the school the Muso Jikiden Eishin-ryu and organized it into its present three-level system. These three sets of waza, *Seiza no Bu* (Omori-ryu), *Tate Hizano Bu* (Eishin-ryu), and *Oku Iai* (*Zawaza* and *Tachiwaza*), along with several sets of partner practice (*Tachi Uchi no Kurai* and *Tsume Ai no Kurai* being the most common) and various leftover katas, total almost one hundred techniques in all.

At the time of the eleventh headmaster, the school had split into two lines, the Shimomura and the Tanimura. The Tanimura line became associated with the "common" folk, or the *goshi* farmer/warriors of Tosa prefecture, while the Shimomura stayed closer to the samurai classes in Kochi, the capital. Both lines were still quite secretive about their teachings when Nakayama Hakudo (1869-1958) was invited to Tosa from Edo. Nakayama studied under teachers from both branches of the Muso Jikiden Eishin-ryu and is considered by some to be the last headmaster of the Shimomura-ha. Eventually he developed a school of iai which has become known as the Muso Shinden-ryu, now centered around Tokyo. It is Nakayama who popularized the name iaido which appeared in 1932. The Muso Jikiden Eishin-ryu has since become more open and is still practiced mainly in the west and south of Japan.

These two contemporaries, Oe Masamichi and Nakayama Hakudo, are largely responsible for the survival and growth of iaido in modern times. The two schools teach similar techniques, the katas differing in interpretation more than in fundamentals. The Muso Jikiden Eishin-ryu has eleven Omori-ryu techniques (with one variation that is seldom practiced) while the Muso Shinden-ryu has added this variation to the set for a total of twelve.

The names used for the individual *waza* are different for each school. At the Eishin-ryu and Oku Iai levels of training, both the names and the numbers of techniques are the same. The Muso Shinden-ryu calls the three levels of practice *shoden* (initiation), *chuden* (intermediate) and *okuden* (hidden or advanced).

The All Japan Kendo Federation (*Zen Nihon Kendo Renmei*, or ZNKR), which is now the largest governing body for iaido schools, released a set of seven *waza* to be studied by kendo students. These techniques were developed by instructors from five different iai schools and represented three *seiza*, one "raised knee" and three standing kata. The set was named the *Sei Tei Gata* which means roughly "representative forms." Students from all ZNKR schools study these techniques as well as those of their own school.

In 1980 three more standing waza were added to *Sei Tei* to enable it to more completely represent the strikes and movements of iaido.

The *Zen Nihon Iaido Renmei* (ZNIR) was formed as an umbrella organization many years before the Kendo Federation introduced iaido. The ZNIR is currently headed by Fukui Torao, the headmaster of the Muso Jikiden Eishin-ryu. This iaido organization also represents many different schools and it has a set of five representative forms called *Iaido Toho* (sword arts).

In recent years several groups have split off from the ZNIR and the ZNKR. These include the *Dai Nihon Iaido Renmei* (DNIR) which has added two more katas to *Iaido Toho*, and the *Iai Giri Do* organization which has incorporated cutting practice into its curriculum. There are doubtless many other organizations in Japan and in the West.

PART ONE
The Techniques of Iaido

An iaido kata is practiced alone and consists of four main elements: a simultaneous draw and cut (*nuki tsuke*), a finishing cut (*kiri tsuke*), the cleaning of the blade (*chiburi* or shaking off the blood), and the return to the scabbard (*noto*). A performance of iaido must show perfect awareness of the surroundings from the moment the student enters the dojo until he leaves. Throughout a particular kata the student must demonstrate unwavering concentration; a feeling of *seme* (literally "attack" but also meaning a spiritual and mental pressure on the opponent) must always be directed toward the imaginary opponent (*kasso teki*) even when the particular motion being performed is relaxed.

TECHNIQUE 1: Oku Iai

The first technique shown here is from the oldest teaching of the school,[3] the *Oku Iai Tachi Waza* (standing techniques). The fifth kata in the set is called *Shinobu* (stealthily) or *Yodachi* (night sword) and is one of the more difficult to understand without explanation. On seeing the kata demonstrated, most people are puzzled, but if it is explained that this kata is used when one is in a dark room with an enemy, its application becomes clear. On suspecting an intruder, the swordsman moves forward and to his left with all senses alert, while drawing the sword (Figs. 1a and 1b).

From this position to one side, he taps the floor with his sword (Fig. 1c). The enemy, hearing the noise, cuts downward to where he thinks his target stands. The swordsman, hearing the swing of the sword, now knows where the attacker is and cuts him down (Figs. 1d and 1e).

Afterward the sword is shaken clean of blood (Fig. 1f) by a strong movement to the side and replaced in the scabbard (Fig. 1g). With care, the swordsman returns to his original position.

The techniques of Oku Iai are direct, fast, efficient and quite dangerous for a beginner. They are not usually taught until after several years of training at the lower levels. The sheathing includes a very fast movement to seat the sword in the scabbard so that it may be drawn again on a moment's notice. There is no assumption that other enemies will not appear.

(Shodan Chris Nunam demonstrating)

TECHNIQUE 2: Tatehiza No Bu

The Eishin-ryu represent katas that were developed by Hasegawa Eishin. The first in the set, *Yoko Gumo* (horizontal clouds), is the most representative of the entire school. The raised-knee starting position (*tatehiza*, Fig. 2a), horizontal draw and cut (*nuki tsuke*), vertical finishing cut (*kiri tsuke*), and the horizontal movement to shake off the blood (*chibun*) are the most common movements or positions in the school. The set breaks down exactly into the four sections of a kata. When executing *nuki tsuke*, the swordsman draws and in the same movement cuts horizontally across the opponent's chest while stepping forward with the right foot (Figs. 2b and 2c).

As the sword comes clear of the chest, the swordsman raises the blade overhead (Fig. 2d) and cuts down through the opponent's head and body (Fig. 2e). The swordsman shifts forward at this point if it is necessary. The sword is now snapped out to the side in *chiburi* and then returned to the scabbard. As the blade is sheathed, the right foot is drawn back to the left heel (Fig. 2f). The swordsman then stands up and returns to the original sitting position.

(Shodan Carole Gallian demonstrating)

Everything about this set of techniques emphasizes its middle position between Omori-ryu and Oku Iai, yet it contains some of the most difficult movements in the entire school. Oe Masamichi developed a method of practicing this set called *haya nuki* (fast draw), which consists of executing all ten waza one after the other with no pause between them. This method is also executed using only one hand for all finishing cuts.

TECHNIQUE 3: Seiza No Bu

The most recent katas to be added to the main Muso Jikiden Eishin-ryu practice are those of the Omori-ryu. It is this set, which begins from the formal seated posture (*seiza*), that draws the most criticism by advocates of the "battle ready" iaijutsu styles. The kata that perhaps best represents the core idea of iaido is *Nuki Uchi* (draw and strike). Beginning in the formal seated posture (Fig. 3a), the swordsman draws the blade (Fig. 3b) and raises it overhead while keeping the body covered. Without pause, he cuts down through the opponent's body, using a spreading motion of the knees to give added weight to the strike (Fig. 3c). After *chiburi* and *noto* (Fig. 3d), the swordsman sits back once again in the formal seated posture.

This kata consists of nothing more than a draw and a strike, and it shows the art of iai stripped of all but its essential element. Perhaps because this kata so embodies the Japanese ideal of simplicity, Muso Jikiden Eishin-ryu contains five slightly different versions of this fundamental movement, one each in Omori and Eishin-ryu and three in Oku Iai.

(Shodan Bob MacMaster demonstrating)

TECHNIQUE 4: Other Katas

There are other techniques which exist in the Muso Jikiden Eishin-ryu that are not part of the core curriculum. One such was developed by Takemura Shizuo, a student of Oe Masamichi (Jones 1989), and is called *Sodesuri Komi* (coming close and touching the sleeve). In this most recent of the katas so far discussed, the swordsman is walking with an enemy on his left-hand side. This is a most dangerous situation because it is difficult to draw and cut on this side without having the sword hand or the *saya* grabbed. As the two walk along, the swordsman grasps his blade and accelerates in front of the opponent (Fig. 4a). As he does this he draws, then puts the blade back to his left side (Fig. 4b). On accelerating away from the opponent, the swordsman draws the edge of the blade across the opponent's lower back to cut the kidneys or across his right triceps to prevent him from drawing his blade (Fig. 4c). As the sword comes free, the swordsman turns to his left rear to face the enemy (Fig. 4d) and cuts him down with a decisive downward stroke (Fig. 4e). *Chiburi* and *noto* follow.

There are several other katas, most executed from the standing position, which are practiced by some in the school but which are not strictly part of the curriculum. These variations and innovations come out of the final level of practice[4] as certain swordsmen contribute their unique understanding to the arts.

The twentieth headmaster, Kono Hakuren, developed a set of nine katas (and two variations) called the *Batto Ho* in the early part of this century which is often taught after Omori-ryu and before Eishin-ryu in the ZNIR schools. This set is not commonly practiced in the ZNKR organization.

(Yodan Kim Taylor demonstrating)

MUSO JIKIDEN EISHIN -RYU — LINEAGE CHART

1. Hayashizaki Jinsuke Shigenobu (1543-1621)

2. Tamiya Heibei Shigemasa

3. Nagano Muraku Kinrosai (Juro Zaemon)

4. Momo Gubei Mitsushige

5. Arikawa Shozaemon Munetsugu

6. Banno Dan'emon No Jo No Busada

7 Hasegawa Chikaranosuke Eishin (Hidenobu). (Headmaster 1610)

8. Arai Seitetsu Kiyonobu

9. Hayashi Rokudayu Morimasa (1661-1732)

10. Hayashi Yasudayu Seisho (d. 1776)

11. Oguro Motoemon Kiyokatsu (d. 1776)

Tanimura-Ha	Shimomura-Ha
12. Hayashi Masu no Jo Masamari (d. 1818)	12. Matsuyoshi Teisuke Hisanari (d. 1808)
13. Yoda Manzai Yorikatsu (d. 1809)	13. Yamakawa Kyuzo Yukikatsu (d. 1848)
14. Hayashi Yadayu (Seiki) Masayori (d. 1823)	14. Shimomura Moichi Sadamasa (d. 1877)
15. Tanimura Kamenojo Yorikatsu (d. 1862)	15. Hosokawa (Gisho) Yoshimasa (d. 1923)
16. Goto Mogobei Masasuke (d. 1898)	16. Nakayama Hakudo (1869-1958)
17. Oe Masamichi Shikei (1852-1927)	
18. Hogiyama (Okiyama) Namaio	
19. Fukui Harumasa	
20. Kono Hakuren (Minoru)	
21. Fuki Torao	

PART TWO
The Genealogy of the
Muso Jikiden Eishin-ryu

The information contained in this history has been gathered from many secondary sources and they do not, by any means, always agree with one another. Any inaccuracies in this information must, therefore, be laid at the doorstep of the author, who does not have access to the primary source materials. The bulk of this history may be found in Warner and Draeger (1982), Draeger (1973a, 1973b, 1974), Jones (1989), Mears (1990), and Shewan (1983). Another valuable source is Iwata (1990). Because the *omote gei* or main subject of the samurai was always *kenjutsu*, the other arts being secondary, there are few stories of famous iai masters. Those figures who were good at both iai and kenjutsu were always better known for their *ken*.

Although iai is assumed to have started in the Nara or early Heian period, it is generally accepted that it was developed fully in the Sengoku Jidai (the age of war 1482-1558). In that period it was necessary to draw the sword quickly if one lost one's spear or naginata, in order to continue fighting. In this era, iai was definitely an art of "quick draw" and the timing was *Go no Sen no Waza*. This means that the draw was made after being attacked. Later the timing was changed to *Sen Sen no Waza* (drawing as the opponent formed the intention of attacking) because having the sword in the scabbard (*saya no uchi*) when one was physically attacked, meant one had a poor chance of winning the fight. During this period there was an increase in the use of infantry tactics as opposed to cavalry. Fighting on foot meant fighting with the spear in massed formations. The *tachi* became a bother if it hung from a cord so it was often inserted into the *obi* (belt), at first with the edge down. Later men started to wear the sword with the edge up and sword smiths began to change the curve of the blade to allow a better draw. This led to the development of the *uchi-gatana* which eventually became the katana.

The gun was accidentally introduced to Japan on the island of Tanegashima by the Portuguese in 1543, just about the time that Hayashizaki Jinsuke was born. Within a very few years many daimyo adopted the weapon as their main offense. Its use against foot soldiers was well demonstrated by Oda Nobunaga against the cavalry of the Takeda at the Battle of Nagashino. The Momoyama era saw the birth of surprisingly modern armies and tactics and a de-emphasis on the *tachi* as a battlefield weapon. All these factors had their effects on the development of iaido.

1) Founder: Hayashizaki Jinsuke (Kansuke) Shigenobu

Hayashizaki Jinsuke Shigenobu is said to have lived around 1543-1621, but his actual birth and death dates are uncertain. Although the art of drawing the sword had been taught since the mid-1500's in such schools as the Katori Shinto, the Takenouchi and the Tatsumi-ryu, Hayashizaki's influence on the art is overwhelming.

Jinsuke is thought to have been born in Tateoka Oshu (Murayama-Shi in Yamagata-Ken) although others say Sagami (now Kanagawa city). He traveled to the village of Hayashizaki in Oshu when he was fourteen, where he prayed to Hayashi Myojin and received divine inspiration for his sword art. Jinsuke spent many years in Bushu and practiced austerities at the Hikawa Shrine from 1595 to 1598. While there he lived at the home of his nephew, Takamatsu Kambei Nobukatsu, who was also Jinsuke's student and founder of the Ichinomiya-ryu.[6] Jinsuke called his sword drawing art the Shinmei Muso-ryu, *muso* in this case referring to the dream which inspired him.

Other names which have been used for his art include the Shin Muso Hayashizaki-ryu, Jushin-ryu, Shigenobu-ryu, Hayashizaki-ryu, Hayashizaki Shigenobu-ryu, and the Hayashizaki Jinsuke Shigenobu-ryu. *Jushin* is an alternative reading of *Shigenobu*. At this time, the general term for drawing the sword was *batto jutsu*. The art of Jinsuke included two different styles of iai, and he practiced with both a 3.3 *shaku tachi* and a 9.5 *sun koshigatana*. These techniques used a *Go no Sen* timing. (Note: one *shaku* = approx. 11.9").

In 1616 or 1617, at the age of seventy-three, Jinsuke went on a *Musha Shugyo* (a period of travel and practice) from which he never returned. It is assumed that he died in about 1621. Jinsuke was enshrined at the Hayashi Myojin Shrine in Yamagata Prefecture, where there is a wooden statue and a sword which is supposed to have belonged to him.

2) Tamiya Heibei Shigemasa (Tamiya-ryu)

The second headmaster in the Jikiden lineage was from the Kanto region and was Tamiya Taira no Hyoe Narimasa, the founder of the Batto Tamiya-ryu. Tamiya was born in Iwamurata, Joshu (Gumma), in the late 1500's. He studied under Toshimoto Moriharu and later under Jinsuke.

Tamiya was an instructor to Ieyasu (1542-1616), Hidetada (1578-1632) and Iemitsu (1604-1651), the first three Tokugawa Shoguns. Tamiya-ryu swordsmen served both the Tokugawa and the Ikeda families for many generations. Tamiya's son, Tsushimamori Nagakatsu, served with Ikeda Terumasa at Amagasaki Castle during the Osaka campaign of 1614. It was Nagakatsu who

31

named the school the Tamiya-ryu. Nagakatsu's student, Wada Heisuke Masakatsu, founded the Shin Tamiya-ryu and Heisuke's "grandstudent," Tsuji Getten, founded the Mugai-ryu. Another of Nagakatsu's students, Eda Yoshizaemon, began the Tamiya Shinken-ryu. Both Tamiya's son and grandson were bodyguards to the Shogun. The Shin Tamiya-ryu became firmly established in the Mito Han, which was to play a large role in the early stages of the collapse of the *bakufu* in the mid-1800's.

3) Nagano Muraku Kinrosai (Jurozaemon) (Muraku-ryu)

Nagano was a student of Tamiya Heibei's. He was a general for the Shinano no Kami family that held Minowa Castle in Joshu. When this family was dispersed by the Takeda, Nagano wandered for a while, possibly studying with Jinsuke. Nagano eventually attached himself to Li Naomasa and was well over ninety when he died. Although Nagano was a top iaidoka, he did not, in fact, run a school or claim any headmastership. As a top-level samurai, he had no need to do so, but people did study his techniques and learn from him. One of these students was Ichinomiya Sadayu Terunobu, the founder of the Ichinomiya-ryu.

4) Momo Gumbei Mitsuchige

No information is available at this time.

5) Arikawa Shozaemon Munetsugu

In the book *Shinden-ryu* (quoted in Iwata 1990), the author states that Arikawa served Toyotomi Hideyoshi (1536-1598).

6) Banno Danuemon No Jo Nobusada (Hanawa)

Banno taught in Edo and was teacher to one of the most important headmasters of the style. The Shinden-ryu states that Banno also served Hideyoshi.

7) Hasagawa Chikaranosuke Eishin (Hidenobu)
Headmaster in 1610 Muso Hasagawa Eishin-ryu

The seventh headmaster in the Jikiden lineage, Hasegawa Chikaranosuke Eishin, was born either in Kochi (Tosa), Tokyo or Nagoya. He studied under the sixth headmaster, Banno Danuemon no Jo Nobusada (Manno Danueimon Nobumasa), in Edo. One source (Warner and Draeger 1982) states that this was during the Kyoho Era (1716-1735), but this does not correspond well with other dates that indicate Eishin becoming the headmaster in 1610, the ninth headmaster succeeding him in 1675, and the eleventh in 1742 (Jones 1989). It is much more likely that Eishin studied in the Keicho (1596-1615).

The book *Muso Jikiden Eishin-ryu Iai Heiho – Chi no Kan* (earth chapter) quotes Hayashi Rokudayu's *Hiden Sho* as stating that this style was called Muso Jikiden at this time. Another Shinden-ryu history states that the art was known as the Muso Shinden Eishin-ryu Batto Heiho. When the lineage moved to Tosa prefecture, the art became known as Hasegawa Eishin-ryu (Iwata 1990).

The Shinden-ryu states that Eishin served the Daimyo Oshu and that he held a castle with an income of 1,000 *koku*. (Note: *koku*, a measure of grain roughly equivalent to 5.2 bushels). He was said to have demonstrated in front of Hideyoshi the matchless techniques or *muso*. This term was taken by Eishin's students to name the school the Muso Hasegawa Eishin-ryu.

Eishin transformed the iai techniques and is said to have devised the style of drawing with the blade edge up in the *obi*. He added his *Iai hiza* (*tate-hiza*) techniques to the Muso-ryu waza. This set is now commonly called the Eishin-ryu.

Some say Eishin left Edo and traveled to Tosa (Kochi) in Shikoku. Hasegawa's early years are a bit of a mystery and some scholars believe that he was the nineteenth headmaster of the Muso Jikiden-ryu (Draeger, 1973b), who later passed the teachings on to his younger students. We should perhaps think of its development as a joint effort by several senior swordsmen. Each of these men may have looked to Jinsuke for the original inspiration but each would also have contributed his unique insights. This early period of development seems to have ended with Eishin and his reorganization of the school. From this point, the headmasters follow from generation to generation. It is this "fixing" of the style which would likely have led to its being called the Muso Jikiden Eishin-ryu in later years.

8) Arai Seitetsu Kiyonobu, Shinmei Muso-ryu

Arai taught in Edo, presumably after Eishin went to Tosa. The fact that the school was sometimes called by its original name, the Shinmei Muso-ryu, may indicate that the art was still "settling down" after Eishin's changes. Arai was said to be quite a scruffy character and a *ronin* (an unattached samurai).

9) Hayashi Rokudayu Morimasa (1661-1732), headmaster in 1675

Hayashi Rokudayu Morimasa, the ninth headmaster was a cook and pack horse driver[7] for Yamanouchi Toyomasa, the Tosa daimyo, while he was at Edo (Tokyo). Hayashi studied the Shinkage Itto-ryu (of the Mito Han). He was also a student of Arai Setatsu Kiyonobu the eighth headmaster of the Shinmei Muso-ryu. Hayashi studied Shinkage-ryu kenjutsu with the ronin Omori Rokurozaemon Masamitsu. When he became the ninth headmaster, he began to teach the Omori-ryu *seiza iai*. Up to this point, the Muso Hasegawa Eishin-ryu only contained techniques which began from *iai hiza* (*tatehiza*, one knee raised) and *tachi waza* (standing). This set became the initiation to iaido. Hayashi eventually returned to his home in Tosa, where he finally and firmly establishing the three iai streams: Shinmei Muso-ryu, Muso Hasegawa Eishin-ryu and the Omori-ryu in Shikoku. These became loosely known as Tosa Iai.

Hayashi wrote a book entitled the *Hiden Sho*, which outlines the history of the school. It is most likely here that the lineage of the first eight head-masters was established for the first time. If so, it would explain the presence of several contemporary headmasters. The Hayashi family was to have a great influence on the school for the next several generations and the main line is traced through them. Hayashi did not call himself headmaster, having no need for a title or a school. He was a high ranking retainer and a well accomplished man, the master of many arts.

10) Hayashi Yasudayu Masanobu (d. 1776)

Yasudayu was the second son of a medical doctor, Dogen Yasuda. He was adopted (*yoshi*) by Hayashi Rokudayu and inherited his estate. Yasudayu had three other students of note beside Oguro, the next headmaster. One student, Mazume Gonosuke Tomone (1748-1807), had an allowance of 200 *koku*. He is said to be the man who brought sugar to Tosa. Kosaka Sennojo and Shibuya Waheiji (d. 1772) were the other two students.

11) Oguro Motoemon Kiyokatsu (d. 1790), headmaster in 1742

Oguro was Yasudayu's son-in-law and student. He had an estate of 250 *koku*. Oguro was said to have studied under Omori Masamitsu although this is difficult to believe since Omori must have been a very old man at the time and there is no indication that he ever traveled from Edo to Tosa. With Oguro's death, a split of sorts began to develop in Muso Jikiden-ryu as Oguro had two very talented students who both passed on their teachings. The split is often assumed to have run roughly along country/city, or *goshi/samurai* lines, a situation which would have developed due to Tosa's somewhat unique administrative organization.

TANIMURA LINEAGE

Since this line of descent involves the Hayashi family, it is taken as the direct line. This opinion differs from that of Warner and Draeger (1982) and others who are influenced by the Tokyo-based Muso Shinden-ryu teachings, which came out of the Shimomura-ha line described later.

12) Hayashi Masunojo Masamori (d. circ. 1815), headmaster in 1799

Hayashi Masunojo Masamori was the grandson of Hayashi Rokudayu's eldest son, that is, the great-grandson of the ninth headmaster. Masamori was a student of Oguro and also of Matsuyoshi Teisuke Hisanari, another of Oguro's top pupils. Matsuyoshi is considered to be the twelfth headmaster of the line which came to be called the Shimomura-ha.

If Masamori became headmaster in 1799 and Oguro died in 1790, there is a gap of nine years. This gap may help to explain why two lines developed. Matsuyoshi Hisanari died soon after Oguro (in 1808) and so might have had a good claim to being the next headmaster, being a contemporary of Oguro and senior student to Hayashi. This would also give the Shimomura-ha line a claim to being the "main line." The debate between "family" and "talent" in the leadership of martial art schools is an old and respectable one.

13) Yoda Manzai Yorikatsu (d. 1809)

Little is known about Yoda except that he was quite poor. His death date also seems a little out of sync with his placement within the lineage. Yoda may have taught Yamakawa Kyuza Yukikatsu, the thirteenth headmaster of the Shimomura-ha.

14) Hayashi Yadayu (Seiki) Masayori (d. 1823)

Hayashi Masayori taught swordsmanship at the Chidokan Dojo in Kochi, Tosa. He was, perhaps, also a student of Yamakawa Kyuzo Yukikatsu, thirteenth headmaster of the Shimomura-ha. Masayori's younger brother and student, Hayashi Hachiroji (d. 1831), later changed his name to Ikeda Wadao. Masayori also taught Ikoma Hikohachi and Tanahashi Saheida.

15) Tanimura Kamenojo Yorikatsu (d. 1862)
Tanimura-ha Tosa Iai, flourished 1844

Tanimura taught *bajutsu* (horse-riding) at the Chidokan Dojo and was a student of Hayashi Masayori. Since Tanimura was an instructor at the prefectural martial arts hall, it might be a bit overly romantic to assume that the line was being carried on by the *goshi*, stamping about up in the mountains. There was obviously close contact between the two lines of the school.

One of Tanimura's students was Yamauchi Yodo (d. 1872) the Tosa Daimyo (Yamanouchike), an advisor to Tokugawa Keiki the last Shogun. Yodo advised Keiki to yield power and avoid a bloody civil war during the final days of the Shogunate.

16) Goto Mogobei Masasuke (d. 1898)

Goto had several students, including Tanimura Noryu, Taguchi Shisen, Sakamoto Masaemon and Morimoto Tokumi. Morimoto in turn taught Takemura Shizuo and Nakayama Hakudo.

17) Oe Masamichi Shikei (1852-1927)

Although Oe followed the teachings of Goto, he was also taught by Shimomura Sadamasa (d. 1877, fourteenth headmaster of Shimomura-ha) and by Shimamura Ummanojo Yoshinori, another Shimomura-ha swordsman. This is a fairly recent example of the interconnection between the two Tosa Iai lines, and perhaps there should be less emphasis on the differences between them. The Muso Shinden school which later developed from the teaching of Nakayama Hakudo (sixteenth headmaster of the Shimomura-ha was, in the beginning, quite close in style to the modern Muso Jikiden Eishin-ryu. Nakayama was himself a student of teachers from both lines.

In the Taisho Era (1912-1926), as the seventeenth headmaster (Tanimura-ha), Oe Masamichi reorganized the school and officially incorporated the Omori-ryu iai waza as the shoden level. Shikei is the man who finally named the school the Muso Jikiden Eishin-ryu and established its present three-level system. He also invented the Haya Nuki practice of the Eishin-ryu, which is done when time is short.

Amongst Oe's students were Masaoka Ikkan, Nishikawa Baisui, Koda Moryo, Matsuda Eima, Yamazaki Yasukichi, Nakanishi Iwaki, Taoka Tsutomu, Suzue Yoshishige, Mori Shigeki, Yamamoto Takuji, Takemura Shizuo, Sakamoto Tosami, Yamauchi Toyoken, Yamamoto Shumske (Harusuke), Fukui Harumasa, and Hogiyama Namio.

Oe died at seventy-four of stomach cancer. The lineage is debated after this point, but the school's credentials have been handed on and the head-masters are as follows.

18) Hogiyama (Okiyama) Namio

No information is available at this time.

19) Fukui Harumasa

Fukui was the last headmaster to live exclusively in Tosa.

20) Kono Hakuren (Minoru), Yamamura-ha

Kono is famous as the man who took Muso Jikiden Eishin-ryu out of Tosa and spread it into other parts of Japan. He is especially well known in the Osaka area where he taught extensively. Kono was headmaster up until the early 1970's.

Shortly after the Second World War, Kono approached the All Japan Kendo Federation about including iaido in its curriculum. The federation at that time was not much interested and wished to concentrate on kendo. As a result, Kono formed the All Japan Iaido Federation, which is now headed by Fukui Torao. Many years later the ZNKR decided to include iaido and the Kendo Federation is now arguably the more influential organization, especially outside Japan.

21) Fukui Torao

Fukui Torao of Gifu-ken is the present headmaster of the Muso Jikiden Eishin-ryu and head of the All Japan Iaido Federation. There is some discussion about just who should have been headmaster after Oe and it has even been suggested that Oe's wife unknowingly gave the lineage papers to Hogiyama, a family friend, in a box with other items. Regardless of this discussion, a more important split in the lineage has occurred due to the existence of two national organizations governing iaido, the All Japan Kendo Federation (ZNKR) and the All Japan Iaido Federation (ZNIR). There is no doubt that the Muso Jikiden Eishin-ryu practiced in these two organizations is stylistically distinct. The differences are not as great as between Jikiden and Shinden, but if the situation continues, the split will widen. It is, therefore, encouraging that there is now talk of a unification of the two organizations.

THE SHIMOMURO-HA LINEAGE

12) Matsuyoshi Teisuke (Sadasuke) Hisanari (d. 1808)

Matsuyoshi was a student of the eleventh headmaster, Oguro Kiyokatsu.

13) Yamakawa Kyuzo Yukikatsu (d. 1848)

Yamakawa may have been a student of the thirteenth headmaster of the Tanimura-ha, Yoda Yorikatsu, as well as of Matsuyoshi. He opened a sword school and one of his students was Tsubouchi Seisuke Chojun. He was also an instructor to one of Tsubouchi's students, Shimamura Ummanojo Yoshinori (died in 1870 at fifty-five). Shimamura in his turn was one of the teachers of Oe Masamichi.

14) Shimomura Moichi Sadamasa (d. 1877), Shimomura-ha Tosa Iai

It is fairly certain that Shimomura taught Oe Masamichi, the seventeenth headmaster of the Tanimura-ha. Shimomura opened a school of iai in 1852. He worked for the Yamanouchi family (the last Daimyo of Tosa) as an iaijutsu and a taijutsu instructor. Another student was Yukimune Sadayoshi (died in 1914 at sixty-five), a high school gatekeeper in Kochi city. Yukimune often demonstrated with De Masamichi and was said to be so skilled that, despite his lowly position, he was the one the audience watched. Two of Yukimune's students were Hirota Kosaku and Soda Torahiko.

15) Hosokawa (Gisho) Yoshimasa (d. 1923 at 75?)

Hosokawa was governor of Tosa and once demonstrated iai for the emperor. He was seven years older than De Masamichi. Although Hosokawa was the first son of Shimamura Yoshinori, he was a student of Shimomura Sadamasa. Hosokawa was known for the power of his iai, and once cut a candle wick, which remained lit. Hosokawa also used to practice cutting downward so as to just touch a grain of rice placed on the dojo tatami.

16) Nakayama Hakudo (Hiromichi) (1869-1958), Muso Shiden-ru

Nakayama was born in Ishikawa Prefecture and was widely studied in iai, kenjutsu, and kendo. He studied the Omori, Muraku and Muso Jikiden Eishin-ryu styles of iaido as well as the Shindo Munen-ryu and other kenjutsu schools.

Both lines of Muso Jikiden Eishin-ryu iai were still quite secretive about their teachings when Nakayama went to Tosa to study under teachers from the two branches. He was a student of the fifteenth Shimomura-ha headmaster, Hosokawa Yoshimasa, and of Morimoto Tokumi Hokushin of the Tanimura-ha. Hakudo applied to Oe Masamichi for instruction but was refused.

Partly because he was told not to teach Muso Jikiden Eishin-ryu to those outside Tosa, Nakayama developed a school of iai which has become known as the Muso Shinden-ryu. It was Nakayama who popularized the name iaido which appeared in 1932. The *muso* in Muso Shinden means "vision" as it did in the original Muso-ryu of Shigenobu while Shinden means "imparted by divine spirit" and refers to the shrine where Jinsuke had his vision. Until 1937 Hakudo used the name "Muso Shinden Batto Jitsu."

Since Hakudo's death there has been no recognized headmaster of the Shimomura-ha or the Muso Shinden-ryu although some candidates have been proposed.

PART THREE
Sword Schools from Jinsuke's Teachings

The following are some of the schools of iaido that arose from Junsuke's teachings. Please refer to the chart on page 43 to establish their relationships.

- Shinmei Muso-ryu *Shin Muso Hayashizaki-ryu*
  f. * Hayashizaki Jinsuke Shigenobu.
  (NOTE: * f. = founder)

Schools Founded by His Direct Students

- Daimyojin Muso-ryu
  f. Takeda Kyobuzaemon Zenshin.
- Hoki-ryu *Batto Hoki-ryu, Ikkan-ryu, or Katayama Hoki-ryu*
  f. Katayama Hoki-no-kami Fujiwara Hisayasu.
- Ichinomiya-yu
  f. Takamatsu Kanmbei/Jinbei Nokubatsu, of Bishu, nephew of Jinsuke.
- Ikkan-ryu *Katayama Hoki-ryu* See Hoki-ryu.
- Jinmei Muso To-ryu
  f. Azuma Shimotsuke-no-kami Motoharu. His student was Sakurai Gorozaemon, whose student was Mirna Yoichizaemon Kagenobu, founder Suio-ryu.
- Muraku-ryu
  f. Nagano Murakusai Shinro or Muraku Nyudo Kinrosai.
- Sekiguchi-ryu
  f. Sekiguchi Yarokuemon Shishin (Jushin). (Sekiguchi Jushin Hachiroemon Minamoto no Sanechika) (1647-1711). This school included a *kumiuchi* (armored wrestling) type *yawara* as well as sword fighting. In the Edo period the school split into separate iaido and jujutsu lines.
- Tamiya-ryu *Batto Tamiya-ryu*
  f. Tamiya Hibei Shigemasa.

OTHER SCHOOLS FOUNDED LATER

- Asaka-ryu
  f. Asaka Yazaemon Katsuchika. From Shinro-ryu from Hoki (Ikkan)-ryu.
- Hayashizaki Shin Muso-ryu
  f. Ohara Moshi Shun-in. Some sources say that this school was founded by Ichinomiya Gonzaemon Katsumon while other sources say that Ichinomiya Gonzaemon Katsumon is actually Ichinomiya Sadayu Teronobu, founder of the Ichinomiya-ryu. From Ichinomiya-ryu, from Muraku-ryu.
- Hayashizaki Tamiya-ryu
  f. Shirai Sobei Naruchika. From Muraku-ryu.
- Higo-ryu *Sekiguchi-ryu Higo-ha*
  f. Izawa Jurozaemon Nagahide. From Shibukawa-ryu, from Kanso-ryu, from Sekiguchi-ryu. Student of Sekiguchi Yurokozaemon (Sekiguchi-ryu Yawara jutsu) and Shibukawa Bongoro (Shibukawa-ryu Iai Jutsu).
- Hijikataha Mugai-ryu
  f. Hijikata Hansaburo. From Mugai-ryu, Shin Tamiya-ryu, and Tamiya-ryu.
- Ichinomiya-ryu *Ichinamiya Koryu*
  f. Ichinomiya Sadayu Teronobu. From Muraku-ryu.
- Ichinomiya To-ryu
  f. Ichinomiya Sadayu Nobutoshi. Perhaps Teronobu's son, perhaps the same person. From Ichinomiya-ryu, from Muraku-ryu.
- Ichinomiya-ryu Tani-ha
  f. Tani Kozaemon Toshimasa. From Ichinomiya-ryu, from Muraku-ryu.
- Ishin-ryu Iai
  f. Suzuki Yoshisada. From Tamiya-ryu.
- Isoyama-ryu
  f. Isoyama Shirozaemon Chikamasa. From Asaka-ryu, from Shinro-ryu, from Hoki-ryu.
- Izawa-ryu
  f. Izawa Gentazaemon Ryoeki. From Hoki-ryu.
- Jiko-ryu
  f. Taga Jikyosei Morimasa. From Tamiya-ryu.
- Jushinshin-ryu
  f. Matsuda Matanojo. From Kanso-ryu, from Sekiguchi-ryu.
- Jushinshin-ryu
  f. Hisase Isaemon Sadakatsu. Perhaps the same person as Matsuda Matanojo.
- Kageyuki-ryu
  f. Yamamoto Hisaya Masakitsu. From Hoki-ryu.

- Kamiizumi-ryu Iai-jutsu *Jasen-ryu/Minya-ryu*
  f. Kamiizumi Magojiri Yoshitane. From Muraku-ryu.
- Kanso-ryu
  f. Sekiguchi Hachirozaemon Ujinari. From Sekiguchi-ryu.
- Kisshu Tamiya-ryu
  f. Tamiya Sunemon. Position uncertain.
- Kubota-ha Tamiya-ryu
  f. Kubota Sukedayu Sei-on. From Tamiya-ryu.
- Mugai-ryu
  f. Tsuji Motoshige Gettan (Sakemochi) (1650-1729). From Shin Tamiya-ryu, from Tamiya-ryu. Tsuji studied Yamaguchi-ryu ken at thirteen. Student of Wada Heisuke of Shin Tamiya-ryu. He established a very popular dojo in Edo in 1676 and founded the Mugai-ryu in 1695.
- Mukei (Muke)-ryu Iai
  f. Bessho Noriharu. From Jiko-ryu, from Tamiya-ryu.
- Muraku-ryu Kamnzumi-ha Iai. Position uncertain; see Kamiizumi-ryu.
- Muso-ryu Iai. See Shinmei Muso-ryu.
- Muso Jikiden Eishin-ryu. From Tosa Iai Tanimura-ha. Name from Oe Masamichi.
- Muso Shinden-ryu
  f. Nakayama Hiromichi Hakudo. From Tosa Iai Shimomura-ha.
- Omori-ryu
  f. Omori Rokurozaemon Masamitsu. From Hasegawa Eishin-ryu, Shinkage-ryu and Ogasawara-ryu Reishiki.
- Sekiguchi-ryu Baito-ha
  f. Katagiri Mokuemon Shigemasa. From Kanso-ryu, from Sekiguchi-ryu.
- Sekiguchi Shinshin-ryu
  f. Watanabe Shirobei Shigekane. From Kanso-ryu, from Sekiguchi-ryu.
- Shibukawa-ryu
  f. Shibukawa Bongoro Yoshinori. From Kanso-ryu, from Sekiguchi-ryu.
- Shimomura-ha Tosa Iai
  f. Shimomura Moichi Sadamasa. From Tosa Iai (Shinmei Muso-ryu, Omori-ryu and Hasegawa Eishin-ryu.)
- Shin Tamiyu-ryu
  f. Wada Heisuke Masakatsu. From Tamiya-ryu.
- Shin-ryu   .
  f. Numazama Jigozaemon Nagamasa. From Muraku-ryu.
- Shin-ryu
  f. Nagai Sakunoemon Hirokata. From Hoki-ryu.

- Shinro-ryu

  f. Takayama Hoki-no-kami Hisakatsu/Yasukatsu. From Hoki-ryu.
- Shinshin-ryu

  f. Sekiguchi Yazaemon Yorunobu/Ujinari. From Kanso-ryu and Sekeguchi-ryu.
- Suio-ryu

  f. Mirna Yoichizaemon Kagenobu. From Jinmei Muso To-ryu.
- Takahashi Hajikyo-ryu

  f. Takahashi Yasuke. From Jiko-ryu, from Tamiya-ryu.
- Tamiya Kanda-ryu

  f. Kanda Shichibei Katsushige. From Shin-ryu, from Muraku-ryu.
- Tamiya Shinken-ryu

  f. Eda Gizaemon. From Tamiya-ryu.
- Tanimura-ha Tosa Iai

  f. Tanimura Kaminojo Yorikatsu (Seiro). (Shinmei Muso-ryu, Omori-ryu and Hasegawa Eishin-ryu.)
- Yamagishi-ryu

  f. Yamagishi Ichiroemon Osasada. From Isoyama, Asaka, Shinro, Hoki-ryu.
- Yamaura-ha Muso Jikiden Eishin-ryu

  f. Kono Hyakuren Minoru (Momonori).

Matsuo Haruna executing *kochibu*ri.
Photo by Bill Mears.

TABLE OF SCHOOLS FROM SHINMEI MUSO-RYU

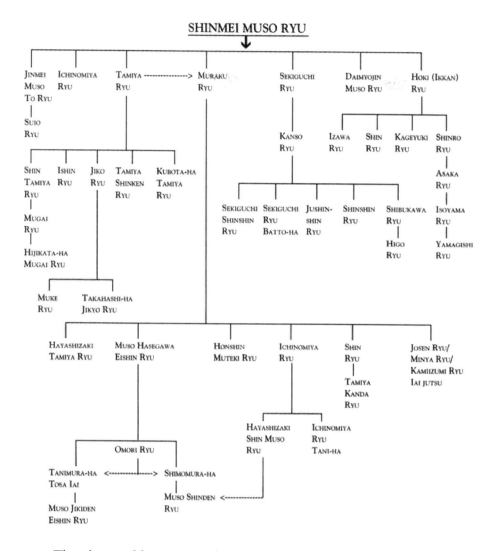

The above table is a genealogy of the various iai schools derived from the teachings of Hayashizaki Jinsuke. A detailed analysis of the history of Muso Jikiden Eishin-ryu and Muso Shinden-ryu has been given. Little has appeared in English about the other schools named here. Note the Muso Jikiden Eishin-ryu below the Muraku-ryu. This school was named by Oe Masamichi after the seventh head, Hasegawa Eishin, although at the time it was more likely called the Eishin-ryu or the Hasegawa Eishin-ryu. Eishin is said to have become seventh headmaster in 1610, while Hayashizaki is thought to have died in 1621.

43

This should not be too confusing if we accept that many of the students of Hayashizaki were actually contemporaries who founded their own schools as seen above. The Eishin line very possibly counted backward from Eishin through his teachers and "grandteachers" to come up with the seventh headmastership. If we accept this we don't have to be overly concerned that during the first few years of the Eishin school, new headmasters were being named while the old were still living. Despite recent North American claims, "lineages" never start with the first "*soke*" (headmaster). They are only established and put into the histories after the school has had several generations of students.

After Eishin the lineage becomes more conventional. The ninth headmaster, Hayashi Morimasa (1661-1732), took the school to Tosa prefecture on Shikoku, where it remained until the twentieth headmaster, Kono Hakuren took it "on the road" in the first half of this century. At the time of the eleventh headmaster, Oguro Motoemon Kiyokatsu (died in 1790), two superior students established two slightly different styles. One was Hayashi Masu No Jo Masamori (died in 1818) who was the great-grandson of Hayashi Morimasa. Masamori's line came to be called the Tanimura-ha after the fifteenth headmaster. Matsuyoshi Teisuke Hisanari (died in 1808) was the other student and he began the Shimomura-ha, named after the fourteenth in that line.

The Omori-ryu had a great influence on both of these lines and the school was eventually absorbed in each. In the table on page 43, the Tanimura-ha is assumed to be the mainline of the Muso Jikiden Eishin-ryu since two of the headmasters before the split were from the Hayashi family and two of the Tanimura-ha headmasters were also Hayashi. The Shimomura-ha ultimately resulted in the Muso Shinden-ryu, which was founded or at least heavily influenced by Nakayama Hakudo.

Conclusion

As more historical information becomes available, the role of Tosa Iai in the development of modern iaido is being clarified. The schools of Muso Jikiden Eishin-ryu and Muso Shinden-ryu are now understood as sister arts in a lineage that was not as deeply divided as previously supposed. The development from Jinsuke's Batto Jutsu to the existing schools of iaido is seen as a continuous line with no abrupt change as the *jutsu* became a "*do*." The difference, if any, is in the intent of the student and the sensei rather than in the art itself.

While the historical work presented in this chapter is far from complete, it does reflect what is currently available in English translation. It is hoped that this framework will provide a good starting point for further research.

Acknowledgement

This work could not have been done without the help of Mr. Goyo Ohmi (godan iaido, rokudan kendo), who translated and explained much of the history. Mr. Fred Y. Okimura (sandan iaido, rokudan judo) provided valuable editorial comments. Also of great assistance was Mr. Bill Mears (sandan iaido), who assembled the genealogy table.

Notes

[1] The term *soke* has come into common usage in the West. In the context of this chapter, *soke* means the headmaster of the school. It does not have the connotation of a family head or of a family succession system.

[2] The terms *bujutsu* and *budo* have usually been defined as meaning those systems of warfare which are practiced for their own sake, as methods of fighing or self-defense (*jutsu*), or as those systems which are practiced mainly for self-improvement (*do*). The writings of Donn Draeger (see Draeger 1973b and Warner and Draeger 1982) have been instrumental in creating this definition. In some cases the *jutsu* are defined as more effective or practical than the *do* which are systems that have been crippled, either through pacifistic ideals or for sporting reasons. In this case, those doing the defining are usually practitioners of a *jutsu*. The case of jujutsu and judo is often cited as support for this definition. In the West the "jutsu" are often arts which have been recently created, usually as a mixture of the more "deadly" techniques of several *do*. The actual historical usage of the terms in Japan would imply that the two terms are largely interchangeable.

[3] The reader should understand that the katas are demonstrated the way they are practiced today. There is no way to know how they were practiced in 1600, but it would be safe to assume that they would look quite different. A martial art is a living thing, and it changes quite naturally through the years, hopefully for the better.

[4] There are three levels of practice for any Japanese art, corresponding to the terms *shu*, *ha* and *ri*. Roughly speaking these are keep, break and leave. The

student first "keeps" or copies the instructor without question, seeking to train the body in the movements and discipline the mind to patience. *Ha* is the process of understanding the movements, of ("breaking" them down and with them, breaking down the relationship between the teacher and the student. This understanding of the movements does not come from the instructor but from the student himself. Words cannot transmit the feeling of a motion; only the correct performance of that motion will do. In the final stage, *ri*, the student understands the essence of the art and must "leave" the teacher. This stage is vital to the health of the art since a teacher whose students do not leave to become more skillful than he, is a teacher who has failed the art. Teachers who "hold back a few secrets" so that they will always be able to beat their students guarantee that their art will die within a few generations.

5 It will do no good if a student simply invents more katas since these will never go beyond his own lifetime. Only a teacher who can pass on his art to those who will pass it on in turn will end up giving a new waza to the school as a whole. For this reason, a kata that is present today will have been developed by a well respected and followed teacher. There is no harm from those who make up new techniques since they usually die out just as quickly. The damage is to the inventor as he wastes his time.

6 There were two "Ichinomiya-ryu" to come from Jinsuke's teachings; the other was founded by Ichinomiya Sadayu Terunobu, who was a student of Nagano Muraku Kinrosai. These two schools and their founders are often confused. Takamatsu's school was not the more popular and may no longer be practiced.

7 What this means, in all likelihood, is that he was something like a quarter-master, in charge of travel and provisions. There is no reason to assume that he was some kind of a super swordsman hiding his light under a basket as he worked in a menial job and practiced late at night as in the movies. He was, in fact, quite a high ranking samurai.

References

Draeger, Donn F. (1973a). *The martial arts and ways of Japan: Vol. 1. Classical bujutsu.* New York: Weatherhill.

Draeger, Donn F. (1973b). *The martial arts and ways of Japan: Vol. 2. Classical budo.* New York: Weatherhill.

Draeger, Donn F. (1974). *The martial arts and ways of Japan: Vol. 3. Modern bujutsu and budo.* New York: Weatherhill.

Iwata, Kenkichi, et al. (1990). Oe Masamichi. *Kendo Nippon Magazine, 11* (9), 34. Translated by Goyo Ohmi. Some other data are also from Kendo Nippon Magazine articles.

Jones, Trevor. (1989, April). A brief history of Iaido. *Kendo News #4*. London: British Kendo Association.

Mears, Bill. (1990). Yugen kan dojo iaido manual. Private publication.

Shewan, Malcolm Tiki. (1983). *Iai: The art of Japanese swordsmanship*. Cannes: European Iaido Federation publication.

Warner, G. and Donn F. Draeger. (1982). *Japanese swordsmanship*. New York: Weatherhill.

• 3 •

How to Watch Iaido
by Nicklaus Suino

Figure 1: The opening attack from the Eishin-ryu
form called *tsuigeki to* (pursuing sword).
All photos of Nicklaus Suino.

Iaido (pronounced: ee-eye-dough) is the traditional Japanese art of drawing the sword. The motions include drawing, blocking, cutting and replacing the sword in the scabbard. Except for perhaps the first five minutes of a demonstration or a demonstration by one of the two or three best swordsmen in Japan, it is not a spectator sport. Even if you practice iaido yourself, you will get bored quite soon watching an ordinary demonstration.

If you ever see one of the best perform his art, however, you have a chance to see something that cannot be duplicated or faked. It is something that will create a small, quiet place in your heart or head that you will never forget. You will find, if you watch carefully and try to remember what you see, that nothing else coming afterwards will ever equal the dry correctness of the actions, and you will wonder how something so undramatic can leave such a powerful impression (Figure 1).

The problem, though, is that you will almost certainly never see the best people perform. I want to help you understand how to watch this art so that, if you ever do get the chance, you won't miss it by being unprepared. Hopefully, you will also learn how to watch for telltale signs of expertise so that you won't be taken in by the many self-proclaimed masters.

Ninety percent of iaido practice is single-person forms. When we practice, we move our bodies and the swords through a set of motions designed to defend against an imaginary attack. We cut and kill the imaginary opponent in all of the more than seventy forms (in the Eishin school), except one. In that form, the opponent is persuaded to retire by placing one's sword against the opponent's wrist just as he is about to draw his own sword. The major cut in all the other forms is often designed not just to cut the opponent, but to completely slice through his body so that it falls into two pieces. The strength of the swordsman and the sharpness of the blade required to cut a person in two is great; therefore, there is almost no room for any variation in the way the cut is performed. It must be done perfectly—from a technical standpoint —and with the entire concentration of the swordsman every time or it is not a legitimate cut.

How horrible! you say. All this talk of cutting people is making you ill. Well, you should also know that most swordsmen these days practice for their entire lifetimes without ever cutting anything, and that the motto of the All Japan Iaido Federation reads; "iaido is not for killing people, but for the preservation of human life. It is a method of cultivating the peaceful man." If this sounds like a contradiction in light of what I wrote in the paragraph above, it may be. Iaido is a typical Japanese martial art in that it advocates peace through martial method. I am not asking you to understand this contradiction, though perhaps if you are a martial arts student you ought to have a close look at it. I just want you to realize that we in the iaido business don't go around cutting people.

Because we don't, however, the art seems decadent to many people. It looks like a form of dancing with the sword: beautiful motions that can be inspiring and in some way represent something done hundreds of years ago but without any meaning today.

Once you see one of the best swordsmen perform, however, you will still be left with a distaste for other exhibitions performed with lesser skills, unless you are exceptionally hard-headed or go with a bad attitude just to prove me wrong. It's not the same feeling you get from a beautiful work of art or a dance, however; at the bottom of it is the thing which lends it its power and dryness. In spite of the fact that iaido somehow teaches people to be more peace-loving and more disciplined, it remains an art built on dealing out death. The only other modern-day art with the same premise is bullfighting, and that is colored by the pride, music and romance of Spain. If you want to understand how bullfighting can be beautiful and inspiring and at the same time be all about death, read Ernest Hemingway's *Death in the Afternoon*. If you understand everything he wrote in that book about bullfighting and apply it to iaido, then you will have gone a long way toward understanding the beauty and power of swordsmanship.

After a number of years of studying with an acknowledged master and practicing every day, I can tell you what makes him (and the few others who nearly equal him in skill) special in two words: no tricks. Every single motion is done in exactly the way it was intended, with a weapon that closely resembles the original Japanese sword, by a swordsman who is fully cognizant of the purpose behind each motion and has trained to be able to perform it. The lack of tricks is difficult enough to understand in bullfighting, where the motions are large and the opponent is clearly visible but much harder to recognize in iaido, which has been distilled by the Japanese love of precision, hundreds of years of refinement, and the fact that there is no visible opponent. By discussing some techniques from a typical iaido form, however, I think I can give you an idea of what to look for when you see a demonstration of the art.

Maegiri, a simple, kneeling form whose name means "Forward Cut," will serve as a good example. The first motion is the draw. The swordsman brings the sword forward out of the scabbard and sweeps it across in front of himself, parallel to the ground, at about the height of his own throat (Figure 2). Applied, the motion is meant to parry the draw of the opponent's sword and, not incidentally, to cut him across the throat. You will understand the stark efficiency of the Japanese swordsman's art when you see that there are no superfluous motions. Every motion has a specific purpose, and usually several deadly purposes.

Figure 2: In *maegiri* (forward cut), the sword must be drawn
straight across the front exactly parallel to the ground.

The sword, of course, is razor sharp and would cut human flesh without much difficulty, but it still requires a certain amount of momentum to do the job. How well the swordsman can turn this drawing and parrying motion into a strong, precise and, therefore, effective cut is one measure of how well he knows his art. There can be no hesitation here; the draw/parry/cut must be done in one motion since the opponent is at the same moment drawing his own sword.

The effectiveness of the motion depends on its precision. The butt of the sword handle is drawn toward the opponent's throat, and when the sword tip clears the mouth of the scabbard it is immediately lifted so that the sword's position is parallel to the ground. That way, when the parrying motion is made, the sword can cut cleanly in a straight line and come to rest in the proper position to begin the next motion. Any angle of the sword will cause inefficiency and weaken the motion, if not cause the attempt at cutting to fail entirely (Figure 3).

Figure 3: Any angle of the sword will
cause inefficiency and weaken the motion,
if not cause the attempt at cutting to fail entirely.

The hardest part of this apparently simple motion, however, is to perform it with strength. When you go to watch a demonstration of iaido, you will probably see a dozen different ways to make this motion appear clean and fast, but if you watch closely you will see that all of them lack strength. The following are some common tricks: making the motion in two parts so that momentum can be added after the sword is placed conveniently in position for the follow-through, leaving out the crucial lifting of the sword tip, performing the motion entirely with the strength of the wrist, or using a sword made of aluminum that is so light a child could wield it convincingly.

Perhaps if you think about the leverage involved, you will understand why it is so hard to wield a sword strongly. The sword is often nearly a meter long, and we are asking for power at the furthest point from the hand, which is itself only about ten centimeters wide.

There are a great number of iaido practitioners who subscribe to the method which advocates placing the hands as far apart as possible on the handle so that they can apply maximum leverage to the blade. These same practitioners often try to use the wrist (and the muscles of the forearm) to make the initial draw and parry we've been discussing. Both techniques try to apply force to a distant point (the tip of the blade) using a lever that is much too small (the handle). Both also isolate the body part used for the force so that the real source of power—which is the body itself, especially the hips and legs—cannot contribute to the equation.

To get a sense of what is required, watch the swordsmen carefully through the drawing motion and then later when they cut. Are the motions of the sword and the body taking place together? They rarely are. That's another way to finesse these motions: to step first, then cut, or even less justifiable, to cut first, then step. Stepping or moving before making the cutting motion is actually a good training method, since the coordination necessary for doing both together is difficult, but it is not the best way, finally, to make a strong cut. Unfortunately, many students of this art don't have the time to practice enough to cut with a unified body movement, or perhaps their teachers never explained it clearly.

To effectively use the long, curved blade of the Japanese sword, one must first remember that things like knives and swords cut best when they are drawn across the object to be cut. The sword is not an axe, and its blade, though extraordinarily strong, is not strong enough to be wielded the same way you would chop with an axe. Yet many people make the mistake of chopping with the blade. The reasons are probably that (1) many books indicate that the sword should be used this way and (2) it's easy to make a nice whooshing sound by whipping the sword tip through the air as fast as possible. Since many practice for years without ever making a real cut, they need to satisfy themselves in some other way, so they try to make a loud noise during the cutting motions (Figure 4).

The correct way is, instead, to turn the hands as close to palm-downwards on the blade as possible, to think about getting power along the entire edge of the blade, and to make a sweeping arc that brings the hands in toward the body near the end of the cut. The arms and sword should move as one unit;

the angle relationship of sword to arms should not change during the cut, which it definitely does if too much wrist is used to drive the cut (Figures 5-6).

Figure 4: Look carefully at the hand positions in this photo, and compare them to Figure 6. Because the sword was shipped through the air instead of properly wielded, the palms end facing upward, the left hand is too high, and the left wrist is bent into an awkward position.

Figure 5: The correct starting position for the cut. The *tsuba* is even with the back of the head, shoulders are pulled down and the wrists direct force strongly through the edge of the blade. The relative angle of the sword and arms should remain the same throughout the cut.

Figure 6: The correct finishing position shows the palms down over the handle, below the body's center of gravity, with both wrists in strong "unbendable" positions.

It is now going to get much more difficult to explain to you what follows unless you pick up a sword and try this for yourself. You'll find that the feeling of cutting through an object is quite different from just slicing through air and is, like many worthwhile things, much more difficult. But if you now find a Japanese *tatami* mat, roll it up, soak it in water overnight and then try to cut it while it stands supported only by a spike at its bottom, you will soon see the merits of the correct method. Or if you have enough money to buy several real Japanese swords, try a cutting technique on a tire hung by a rope. I recommend avoiding steel-belted radials unless you and your sword are very good indeed. Trying to finesse the cut while hitting a tire will destroy your sword and your hands faster than you can believe.

If you've practiced other martial arts, especially karate and aikido, with a good instructor, then you know that nearly all strong body motions involve pushing rather than pulling. A large percentage of the difficult and strange looking motions made by martial artists are for the purpose of getting their bodies into position to deliver some kind of pushing attack or for setting their opponents up to be pushed (or punched, kicked or thrown, all of which are demonstrably different forms of pushes when done correctly). The difficulty in cutting properly with a Japanese sword is that there can be no part of the cut that is anything other than a push.

But if you try an experiment, you'll see that pushing strongly from the positions assumed by the swordsman when he cuts is not easy: stand with one leg well behind the other, in good balance. Move both hands above your head with palms touching and the elbows extended out to the sides. Have a friend block your hands from the front (with one arm, say) and try to push straight ahead and down, as if you were cutting with a sword. Do it slowly so you can get an idea of how little strength you have in this position (Figure 7).

Figure 7: Even though David is leaning forward slightly, he cannot generate any forward force because his elbows are too wide, his shoulders too high, and his hand in a weak position.

If you don't feel weak in that position, try (in the same stance) moving your elbows back until you do feel weak. This is the position from which many amateur swordsmen try to cut. One reason they try to whip the sword down with the wrists is that their arms feel weak in this position and the weakness persists all the way through the cutting motion if it is done incorrectly.

To see what the swordsman must do to make the cut correctly, try the same experiment, but this time change three things: (1) make sure that your shoulders are pulled down rather than raised, (2) turn the palms of your hands forward, and (3) move the elbows slightly forward. Push forward and down along the circular path of the sword cut. Feel any different? If you have a normal human bone structure and normal muscles, it should feel much stronger (Figure 8).

Figure 8: In this photo, David has pulled his shoulders down, moved his elbows forward slightly and opened his palms. He is now able to push strongly forward and down.

That strength you felt when you adjusted your position is the strength the swordsman needs to make a strong cut. He must turn his palms downward onto the back of the handle and use his elbows correctly to deliver power to the edge of the blade while slicing, not hacking, along the arc of the cut. The elbows are held somewhat widely at the top of the cut and brought close together at the bottom. This posture also has the benefit of helping to stop the sword cleanly without using the arm muscles too much, which is practical if you are not actually cutting anything, which is the case for most iaido practitioners. It is quite embarrassing to hit the ground with your blade during an exhibition. It's also bad for the blade.

Many beginning swordsmen employ tricks in order to swing the blade quickly and still avoid hitting the ground. After they've hit the ground once or twice, they become afraid to put any real power into the motion, so they finesse the stopping component of this motion, too, in one of several ways.

The most common way is to hold the hands far apart on the handle and swing the right hand in the larger arc than the left. The sword tip then moves very fast while the handle region moves more slowly (like the inner part of a record on a turntable). The motion can be stopped very easily while still getting a satisfying amount of whistling noise from the blade. This trick deprives the cut of its real power.

You can get a clear idea of how difficult it is to practice iaido correctly if you realize that every motion in every form is meant to serve a specific purpose, and for that reason each has a very particular way it must be done. There are variations among styles, but for the most part these variations do not affect the way the basic cutting and parrying motions are done. If you practice Shindo Munen-ryu, Hoki-ryu or Mugai-ryu, the cutting motion still derives from the same intent: to cut the opponent. And the larger purposes of martial arts training are still the same ones: to make you physically fit, to teach you discipline and concentration, and to make you a better person.

This last point is the most difficult to understand. Here's how it works: If, in your iaido practice, you not only swing the sword around but also think about what purpose the motion has, then you will eventually learn how to do the motion correctly. Any motion, done carefully many times over a period of years, will teach you how to use your body. If you use a trick to get the motion done, then instead of educating your body to perform something real you will be fooling yourself. When the time comes to actually use the motion (there may never be such a time for you to use your sword), you will probably fail. That's why, in all martial arts, we must constantly check our methods to be sure they have some basis in reality. Those checks keep us from self-delusion and offer the best guarantee that the "self-defense" aspect of our training is legitimate.

The practice will help you learn about truth. If the motion has a real application, such as the cutting motion in iaido forms, then there should come a point in your training when you can say, "This and this are not correct. They wouldn't really accomplish the cut (or whatever). Only when I do this in this particular way do I achieve the results I want." You may be wrong, of course, but you won't be if you are really honest about what you are doing, and through your own efforts over a long period of time you will have learned something, a simple truth about one small part of the world. The satisfaction that comes from that should help you realize that it takes a long time to really learn something well and that your earlier opinions about this matter were probably wrong.

Two ideas can help an individual lead a more productive life and can make one more valuable to the human race. If it takes a long time to learn something well, then shouldn't we spend more time studying before we begin to call ourselves experts? And if our earlier opinions on some matter were wrong, then why don't we listen more carefully to the teacher (or look more carefully at the world) before adding our noise to that of the crowd?

Well, you started out reading a chapter on how to watch iaido and ended up getting a bit of Japanese philosophy on living. In the meantime, when you next have a chance to watch an iaido demonstration, look carefully at the participants' form. Do all the motions appear strong? What constitutes a strong motion? What constitutes extra motion in this particular movement? Are those swords really aluminum? (Don't ever ask to handle another person's sword. Just look carefully; the alloy swords are either too shiny-like chrome or they are the color of an aluminum pop can. Appreciation of Japanese swords is another art that can take a lifetime to learn.) If you notice even one trick, it should cause you to question the legitimacy of the whole performance. If you notice no tricks, it may be that you aren't yet well educated about iaido, or it may be that you are actually in the presence of an able swordsman. You should be able to take something profound away from the demonstration though it may not be apparent just at that moment.

Anyway, watching carefully, listening, and waiting to make a judgment until you have all the information are just forms of common sense, right? I'm sad to say that many fellow martial artists don't always display too much of this characteristic, which is why chapters like this one must be written. When we do our jobs right, however, it is pleasant for the rest of the world to watch us and we can help educate people in some of the qualities that martial arts are famous for, besides wearing pajamas during the day and shouting at people. There are, in fact, many worthwhile reasons to study the martial arts. When you see one of those few real masters perform, you'll understand one reason.

• 4 •

Interview with Japanese
Sword Instructor Haruna Matsuo

by Kimberley Taylor, M.Sc., and Ohmi Goyo

Haruna (standing r.) demonstrating with his student, Oshita Masakazu.
Seated left is Gary Hall of Halifax, Nova Scotia; and seated right is
Kimeda Takeshi of Toronto, Ontario. *Photos courtesy of K. Taylor.*

In 1989, Ohmi Goyo was invited to England to practice with Haruna
Matsuo, a Muso Jikiden Eishin-ryu Iaido *sensei* (instructor) who had been
teaching regular seminars in that country for several years. As a result of that
meeting, the University of Guelph Iaido Club invited Mr. Haruna to Canada
the next year. The year 1994 marked Mr. Haruna's fourth visit to Canada.
During this visit, we interviewed him for the *Journal of Asian Martial Arts.*

Along with instructor Haruna, several of his fellow instructors and
students have visited Guelph over the years and we would like to thank them
for their instruction. Special thanks go out to instructor Mano of Japan,
instructor Komaki of Sweden, instructor Ono of Japan; and to Trevor Jones,
currently of Japan, for their help. We would also like to note the help given to
us during these seminars by Kimeda Takeshi of Toronto, whose kindness has
made our Japanese visitors feel more at home.

Iaido is the art of drawing the sword. The word *iai* comes from the phrase
"*tsune ni itte kyu ni awasu,*" meaning "always, whatever you are doing, whether
sleeping, walking, running, or sitting (*tsune ni*)" and "wherever you are (*itte,
iru*)" you must "be ready or be prepared to recreate harmony or balance
(*awasu*)." *Iai* comes from *itte* and *awasu* and is a short way of remembering this
phrase.

Haruna is a seventh degree (*dan*) in kendo and an iaido instructor (*kyoshi*) who resides in Ohara Village, Okayama Prefecture. Accompanying him this year for his second visit to Canada was his senior student, Mr. Oshita Masakazu, seventh-dan iaido instructor. Mr. Haruna is a retired junior high school teacher, a member of the All-Japan Kendo Federation, a director of the Okayama Prefecture Kendo Federation, and chief instructor and director of the Musashi Dojo in Ohara. The Musashi Dojo is owned by the town and is situated beside the Musashi Museum. Mr. Oshita also belongs to the All-Japan Kendo Federation and is a director of the Kobe City Kendo and Iaido Federation, vice director of the Hyogo Prefecture Iaido Club, and chief instructor and manager of the Kobe City Iaido Club. Mr. Ohmi Goyo, sixth-dan kendo, fifth-dan iaido, of Toronto, provided the interpretation for the interview.

Some members of the senior class about to begin a kata.

Left: Haruna correcting the posture of Harry Eastwood of Toronto.
Right: Haruna demonstrates a point while Oshita looks on.

INTERVIEW

KIM TAYLOR: I would like to thank both of you for coming this year to Canada, and for the last few years of instruction in iaido. Haruna Sensei, I would like to start by asking you about your competitive achievements in iaido, I know your career is quite impressive. [Iaido competition is done with the competitors side by side facing a panel of three judges. Five kata are performed and a winner is then declared.]

HARUNA MATSUO: I have participated in 256 provincial and national competitions and demonstrations. Of these, I lost completely twelve times, came in third place eight times and second place twenty-eight times. I was awarded "Best Fighting Spirit" forty-five times and "Special Fighting Spirit" [an award higher than Best Fighting Spirit] fifteen times. The rest I won. I entered my first national competition in 1978 and placed second. Overall at national competitions, I placed in the top eight twice, came third twice, second place five times, and in 1989 I won at the seventh-dan level. This year, I placed second again.

- DO YOU ENJOY COMPETING, SENSEI?

Enjoy it? I can't answer whether I enjoy it or not, but competition is practice.

- TO TEST YOURSELF, TO HAVE A CHALLENGE?

No, I don't practice for competition (*shiai*). Competitions are simply another practice day for me.

- SO PRACTICE AND COMPETITION ARE THE SAME, AND YOU SHOULD HAVE THE SAME ATTITUDE DURING PRACTICE AND DURING COMPETITION?

Yes.

- WHERE DID YOU BEGIN YOUR IAIDO PRACTICE?

My first instructor was Yamashibu Yoshikazu, eighth-dan master (*hanshi*), who died last year. His teacher was Yamamoto Harusuke, who studied under Oe Masamichi, the seventeenth headmaster of Muso Jikiden Eishin-ryu Iaido. I started practice in 1972 at age of forty-six.

- WAS IT DIFFICULT TO START IAI AT THAT AGE?

No.

- HAD YOU PRACTICED OTHER MARTIAL ARTS BEFORE STARTING IAIDO?
I started kendo at the age of sixteen in school.

- DO YOU STILL PRACTICE KENDO?
Of course.

- I KNOW YOU ALSO PRACTICE NITEN ICHI-RYU, DID YOU BEGIN THAT PRACTICE BECAUSE OF THE ASSOCIATION OF OHARA WITH MIYAMOTO MUSASHI? [Niten Ichi-ryu is the sword style of Musashi who was born near Ohara.]
No, not because I am director of Musashi Dojo. Twenty-six years ago, the eighth headmaster of Niten Ichi-ryu, Aoki Tesshin of Kumamoto Province, came to the Musashi Dojo in Ohara. Aoki Sensei felt the headmastership should return to Musashi's home area and the Musashi Dojo, and so came to teach. I joined then. Although many people have suggested that the headmaster should be from Musashi Dojo, so far nobody in Ohara is ready for that position. After Aoki Sensei, Kiyonaga Tadanao became the ninth head but died after a few years. The current head is Masayuki Imai of Oita Province in Kyushu. I visit Imai Sensei every year to study Niten Ichi-ryu.

- I UNDERSTAND THAT THERE ARE TWO BRANCHES OF THE NITEN ICHI-RYU.
Yes, there is the Noda-ha Niten Ichi-ryu and the Hyoho Niten Ichi-ryu, which is headed by Imai Sensei. This school is named the Santo-ha in an old book, but the name is no longer used. The name Santo-ha came from one of the teachers in the lineage. *Hyoho* is written the same as *Heiho* but is properly pronounced Hyoho.

- WHERE DO YOU USUALLY PRACTICE NITEN ICHI-RYU?
In the Musashi Kenyu Club in Ohara. *Kenyu bu* translates as "sword friendship club" and is one of several Niten clubs in the town. About eight members in this club practice at the Musashi Dojo once a week.

- TO POINT OUT HOW LITTLE INFORMATION WE IN THE WEST HAVE ABOUT NITEN ICHI-RYU, I HAVE SOME COMMENTS AND QUESTIONS HERE THAT WERE ASKED ON THE IAIDO-L COMPUTER MAILING LIST. THE FIRST STATES THAT THE QUESTIONER THOUGHT THE NITEN ICHI-RYU WAS NO LONGER BEING PRACTICED.
The Niten Ichi-ryu headmaster is Masayuki Imai and he owns the headquarters dojo. There are branch groups in Okayama, Kumamoto, Fukuoka, Saga, and Saitama Prefectures. There are probably 120-130 people from these clubs

practicing Niten Ichi-ryu in Japan today. I don't know how many people practice under the Noda-ha.

- THE SECOND QUESTION CONCERNS THE CONTENT OF THE SCHOOL.

The Tachi Seiho set consists of practice with the long sword against the long sword. Kodachi Seiho is short sword against long and the Nito Seiho is long and short sword against long sword. These are the three sections of practice. There is also a *bojutsu* or long staff set that is staff against long sword. I have not practiced the bojutsu.

- I HAVE SEEN A VIDEOTAPE OF IMAI SENSEI AND HIS STUDENTS DEMONSTRATING BOJUTSU. IT IS NOT AT ALL THE SAME STYLE OF BO WE WOULD SEE HERE, DERIVED FROM OKINAWAN KARATE.

The Niten Ichi-ryu bo is a little bit longer than the Muso-ryu jodo staff.

- IT SEEMS SIMILAR TO JODO.

Yes, but the specific movements are quite different from Muso-ryu jodo.

- HOW MANY KATAS IN EACH OF THE THREE SWORD SETS?

Tachi Seiho has twelve katas altogether, and Kodachi Seiho has seven.

Haruna Matsuo demonstrates a sword drawing technique and, at right, performing the closing etiquette of the Kendo Federation Iaido set in the main practice hall of the University of Guelph.

- THAT IS THE SET WE HOPE TO LEARN FROM YOU TOMORROW.

That is not possible. It can't be learned in only a couple of days. Don't think so simply [laughing].

- AND NITO SEIHO?

Nito Seiho has five katas.

- ONLY FIVE? ARE THERE ANY OTHER NITO KATAS?

There are five katas called the *Setssusa* (pronounced *sessa*) and five katas called *Aikuchi*. Imai sensei does not teach Sessa and Aikuchi. Aoki Sensei told Imai Sensei that it is not necessary to practice these katas. For instance, I showed you Jinrai and Raiden in the demonstration today. These iaido katas were created for practice only and are not part of the school. Sessa and Aikuchi were not created by Musashi but by later students after he died. Imai Sensei said that it is not necessary to practice them, so we do not. At least not often.

- A FINAL QUESTION FROM THE COMPUTER LIST CONCERNS HOW PEOPLE LOOK AT MUSASHI IN JAPAN. IN THE WEST, WE SOMETIMES GET THE IMPRESSION HE IS A RATHER AMBIGUOUS FIGURE, SORT OF LIKE BILLY THE KID.

The Japanese don't think this way. He's not an outlaw or like Billy the Kid. Most people think of him as a philosopher. Budo people look to him as a philosopher, a writer, and are proud of him for his swordsmanship and for his artistry as a painter and sculptor. There are fictional accounts of his life but most people don't believe these stories.

- THIS CONFIRMS WHAT I HAVE HEARD. FOR INSTANCE, DURING A LECTURE IN NEW YORK CITY LAST YEAR, THE CURRENT HEADMASTER OF THE YAGYU SHINKAGE-RYU REFERRED TO MUSASHI'S BOOK GO RIN NO SHO WHEN EXPLAINING THE DIFFERENT TYPES OF SEEING.

Yes, he is respected for his whole life, as an artist and not just for his skill with a sword.

- MAYBE WE SHOULD GET BACK TO IAIDO. SENSEI, I HAVE A WHOLE SERIES OF TECHNICAL QUESTIONS WRITTEN DOWN HERE BUT YOU HAVE JUST GIVEN US THREE DAYS OF EXPLANATIONS AND I KNOW YOU COULD SPEAK FOR THREE DAYS ON THESE QUESTIONS. PERHAPS YOU COULD COMMENT ON WHAT IS MOST IMPORTANT FOR BEGINNERS TO LEARN.

Beginners should work on the angles of *nuki tsuke* [the one handed opening cut] and on footwork first. If they don't, they will pick up bad habits which are very difficult to fix. Real beginners should not learn katas first but work on the vertical cut only, and on *noto* [putting the blade away], not on the first technique. Even in Japan, beginners go too fast. Many learn the second, third, and fourth techniques too soon and this causes trouble. In the old times, during the first three years they taught students only the first technique. In kendo, they also say one should do *kiri kaeshi* [a basic cutting drill] for three years before putting on the *bogu*. If we do this today, nobody will stay in the class. So we teach techniques from one through ten as soon as possible. I believe that's why most people's iai is very bad. If you do the first kata perfectly, master it completely, there won't be any problem going on to the next kata. Learn breathing, the vertical cut, and the other parts of the first technique fully before going on. The sooner you teach the rest of the techniques, the sooner the beginner gets into trouble. Teach the basics deeply.

• WE'VE MENTIONED WHAT TO TEACH BEGINNERS, WHAT DOES A SENIOR IN IAI DO THAT MAKES HIM DIFFERENT FROM A BEGINNER?
We teach beginners simple movements. For instance [demonstrating], in footwork the teaching is very simple, move the foot, turn. When it comes to a senior, this is not good enough. The movements must be more refined, more subtle. Seniors must be taught the fine technical points of each movement. The movement is broken down into many more steps to teach it deeply.

• SO BEGINNERS AND SENIORS WILL PERFORM THE SAME KATA, THE SAME MOVEMENTS BUT THE SENIORS MUST SHOW MUCH MORE REFINED, CONTROLLED MOVEMENT. JUNIORS PERFORM BIGGER, ROUGHER MOVES. SENSEI WHAT ATTITUDE MUST A STUDENT HAVE FOR COMPETITION, DEMONSTRATION OR TESTING?
The attitude will be no different between these.

• WHAT ABOUT EVERYDAY PRACTICE?
It shouldn't be different. When you do *keiko* [practice] you should do it seriously. For instance, the students did a demonstration for me on the last day of the seminar. During practice, everyone was easygoing and relaxed, but during the last fifteen minutes they thought "now sensei is watching me" so they preformed carefully. That feeling is wrong. You should do *keiko* the same as *embu* [demonstration].

• AT ONE POINT IN THE SEMINAR, I BELIEVE YOU MENTIONED THAT WE SHOULD

Of course you should practice that way. Most people are practicing without this attitude and that's why they're doing it wrong. They have no concentration during practice. The point is: Are you practicing seriously or not? Most people are not serious. If you're not practicing seriously, just go to bed. This is what Tomigahara Sensei [ninth-dan Hanshi, Muso Shinden-ryu] always taught me. In the demonstration, the students all did "*shinken shobu*" [fight with a real sword, a serious attitude] but when practicing they were not serious. There should be no difference in the two feelings.

Haruna Matsuo demonstrates a standing draw.

• SENSEI, DO YOU THINK THAT STUDENTS WHO HAVE GAINED EXPERTISE IN IAIDO SHOULD PRACTICE OTHER STYLES, FOR INSTANCE KENDO?
Of course, iaido students should study kendo as well. The International Kendo Federation has also stated that kendo and iaido should be practiced together. The two are the wheels of a cart. If one wheel is missing, the cart falls over. Most budo experts have this opinion.

• WOULD OTHER STYLES OF KENJUTSU, FOR INSTANCE NITEN ICHI-RYU, HELP IN PRACTICE?
Yes, Niten Ichi-ryu helps iaido a lot. Kendo helps iai and iai helps kendo. Today one of the students told me that iai practice helped her Chinese taijiquan. It is all the same.

• SO YOU BELIEVE THAT THERE IS NO DANGER OF DOING TOO MANY THINGS, OF KNOWING A LITTLE ABOUT A LOT AND NOT BEING GOOD AT ANY ONE THING?

If you do iaido, kendo, or jodo only, this is not good. You should do more than one of these. Other budo, like *kyudo* [archery], have the same "mind" but the techniques are very different. That much diversity is not necessary. I believe you should not learn that much budo.

• SO THE IMPORTANT THING IS THE MIND?

The mind is the same but the techniques are different. Iaido and kendo's mind and technique is the same. If you do one, you should do the other. Kyudo's concentration is the same as iaido's. The mind is the same but the skills and movements are different. *Sado* [tea ceremony], flower arranging, . . . all the *do* [*michi* or ways] have the same mind as budo. They all help the budo. That is Japanese culture.

• SO THE REASON WE DO BUDO IS TO IMPROVE OUR MIND, NOT TO LEARN HOW TO CUT PEOPLE IN HALF WITH A SWORD?

That is the most important part of budo. The technical part of cutting is not important. That is a good question. We must all learn *do*, not only cutting. To go more deeply, the iaido mind must be used in everyday life. From that will follow peace in the world.

• SO, *KATSUJIN KEN* NOT *SATSUJIN KEN*.

Just so, "the sword that gives life, not the sword that takes life."

• THEN YOUR ADVICE IS TO PRACTICE IAIDO, KENDO, AND JODO. THEIR TECHNIQUES ARE SIMILAR AND THEY ALL WORK ON THE MIND. IAIDO AND KYUDO, ON THE OTHER HAND, BOTH WORK ON THE MIND BUT THE TECHNIQUES ARE CONFUSING, SO DON'T PRACTICE THEM TOGETHER?

I believe you can't practice so many different methods. If you are a samurai, you must practice everything, but today people have to make a living. If you do budo all day, that's different. Go ahead and learn kyudo, karate, aikido, judo. Today, nobody can do everything. Stick to kendo, iaido, and jodo, if you must also make a living.

• IN IAI, WHO ARE THE IMPORTANT FIGURES WE SHOULD KNOW ABOUT? SHOULD STUDENTS LEARN ABOUT OE MASAMICHI, HAYASHIZAKI JINSUKE, . . . WHICH OTHERS?

Hayashizaki Jinsuke is the originator of iai techniques and we should know about him. Remember that our iai and Jinsuke's iai is not the same any more. Jinsuke's students created many different schools, and Jinsuke is the head of all of these. You mentioned Oe Masamichi. He is important for Muso Jikiden Eishin-ryu but not for other styles or schools. So when talking about the history of iaido, the most important is Hayashizaki Jinsuke. Then students of a particular school should also know the history of their own school.

• As students of budo, what other figures should we know about and study? Whose lives should we learn from?
The number one figure would be Miyamoto Musashi and his book, *Go Rin no Sho*. This book contains everything, how to hold the sword, *metsuke* [gaze], posture. The book explains mind, spirit, and how to face an enemy in a fight. Musashi wrote the book with reference to fighting, but the writing is alive today. Company managers use it to understand how to manage people. The *Go Rin no Sho* explains how to live your life. It is not only a book on fighting.

• Are there any other books or lives we should study?
The *Go Rin no Sho* is enough.

• What personal characteristics are required to make a good budo practitioner?
Your question is backward. If you practice budo, you develop a good character. Budo improves your character. A baseball coach may be able to say, this person should be good as a baseball player. A budo person will never say, this person shouldn't study budo. Everyone can practice budo and everyone can learn *kokoro* (heart/mind/spirit/personality) from budo.

• What do we learn from budo?
Kokoro. This is difficult to explain. Top sensei often argue about the meaning of *kokoro*. One person said that trying to explain *kokoro* was like trying to tie up a young girl's messy hair; it keeps slipping away. One sensei said *kokoro* is *you*, but where is it? In your arm? No. In your heart? In your mind? *Kokoro* is the whole person.

• What is the relationship between student and sensei?
Student and sensei are walking along together. I am here, that's why the

student is there. The student is there, that's why I am here. If the sensei doesn't think that way, he's not good enough to be a sensei. A bossy, bullying person is not a sensei. If students are polite to a teacher's face, but talk about him behind his back because he's a bully, this shows he's not a good sensei. A good example is Tomigahara Sensei. He's not bossy at all. He's very simple and humble in his actions and that's why I follow him. The sensei's humanity is most important, not his rank.

Left to right: Oshita Masakazu, Haruna Matsuo, Ohmi Goyo (Toronto), and Stephen Cruise (Toronto). At six months, Lauren Taylor was the youngest to attend the seminar. Note the excellent grip.

• UNFORTUNATELY, RANK IS OFTEN THE MOST IMPORTANT THING IN THE WEST. WHAT IS THE RELATIONSHIP BETWEEN STUDENT AND ORGANIZATION THEN?
A relationship between student and sensei makes sense, but a relationship between student and federation doesn't seem to match. What do you mean?

• FOR INSTANCE, WHAT LOYALTY SHOULD A STUDENT GIVE TO A SENSEI AND WHAT LOYALTY TO A FEDERATION?
When a sensei is wrong, for instance if he splits from an organization and that split is wrong, the student has an obligation to tell his sensei that he's wrong and stay with the organization. On the other hand, if the sensei is right to leave the organization, then the student should follow him. The decision of right or wrong lies with the student and the student must decide for himself what to do. A student can't give this decision to the sensei.

• I SUPPOSE THE ANSWER THEN IS THAT A STUDENT HAS A RELATIONSHIP WITH A SENSEI BUT IS MERELY A MEMBER OF AN ORGANIZATION. SENSEI, IS IT POSSIBLE FOR A STUDENT FROM THE WEST TO UNDERSTAND BUDO OR MUST ONE BE JAPANESE TO FULLY GRASP IT?

I believe Western students who practice budo can understand it . . . some of these students understand it. You don't have to be Japanese. Even the Japanese don't understand what budo is [laughs]. Many Japanese, many Americans, many Europeans understand what budo is today.

• SENSEI, YOU HAVE TRAVELED TO THE WEST MANY TIMES. DO YOU ENJOY THESE VISITS?

Yes, I really enjoy the visits. I wish for many people to understand about budo, so I'd like to share all my knowledge about budo with as many people as possible.

• HOW WOULD YOU COMPARE THE SKILL LEVEL OF THE STUDENTS IN THE WEST TO THOSE IN JAPAN?

The technical skill of the West is still quite low compared to Japan. Many Europeans understand the mind of budo but the technical skill is still lower than in Japan. For example, your rank in iaido is only fourth-dan but your knowledge of budo is high. I have a high opinion of your knowledge of budo.

• I PROMISE TO PRACTICE HARDER SENSEI. I WOULD LIKE TO THANK YOU VERY MUCH FOR GIVING ME YOUR TIME LIKE THIS. IT WAS MOST KIND OF YOU TO SHARE YOUR KNOWLEDGE WITH US.

5

The Omori-ryu
A History and Explanation
by Kimberley Taylor, M.Sc., and Ohmi Goyo

Photos courtesy of K. Taylor.

Introduction

Iaido is the art of drawing and cutting, all in the same motion, with the Japanese sword. Mention is made of sword drawing techniques as early as the Heian period (794-1185). The art of iaido in its modern form may have been developed as early as the beginning of the Muromachi era (1338-1573), when paintings show that the sword was often thrust through the sash (*obi*) rather than slung from a suspending cord. The familiar *katana*, the long-sword worn through the sash on the left side, became popular in Japan in the mid-1500's (Sato, 1983: 61-62) and the art of iaido using the katana was developed very shortly after this.

Traditional iaido practice outside Japan today is dominated by two schools, the Muso Jikiden Eishin-ryu and the Muso Shinden-ryu. These are closely related styles that trace their lineage from the beginning of the seventeenth century. The word *ryu* is usually translated as "school," but it should be understood that it more accurately means a lineage, that is, a tradition of study rather than a physical place.[1]

70

The first set of techniques that a student must learn in either the Muso Jikiden Eishin-ryu or the Muso Shinden-ryu are often introduced as "Omori-ryu," which invariably causes confusion. Is it a set within the main school or is it a separate school in itself? One occasionally reads articles by authors who state that they are Omori-ryu swordsmen, and by others who study the Muso Shinden-ryu or the Muso Jikiden Eishin-ryu. This chapter is intended to put the Omori-ryu into its proper place historically.

The Omori-ryu katas are quite often the only introduction people have to iaido and, as such, they have a great influence on what people think of iai. However, due to their unique nature, they may give a false impression of the art. Some discussions from the martial arts literature concerning *iai-do* (*iai* as a "way" of self-development) in comparison to *iai-jutsu* (*iai* as a combative art) will be critically examined from this viewpoint.

The Omori-ryu has also influenced what type of student continues in the art. When asked why they did not return after the first few classes, most people will say they liked iaido but they did not like all the kneeling. Does this mean that beginners should start their iaido practice with standing techniques? Perhaps, if one is seeking lots of students, but it can be argued that this would be doing these students no favor. We will discuss a few of the swordsmanship concepts that are taught in the Omori-ryu.

Omori-ryu

The history of the Omori-ryu is linked with that of several schools, including the Hayashizaki Shinmei Muso-ryu, so the proper starting place is difficult to find (Warner and Draeger, 1984; Jones, 1989; Shewan, 1983; Mears, 1990). We will begin with the Muso Shinden and Muso Jikiden Eishin lines. A detailed discussion of the Shinmei Muso-ryu and associated schools can be found in an earlier issue of the *Journal of Asian Martial Arts* (Taylor, 1993).

The man popularly credited with the origination of iaido is Hojo Jinsuke Shigenobu (also Hayashizaki, or Rinzaki; cir. 1546-1621). Jinsuke Shigenobu was from Yamagata-ken (formerly called Oshu), north of Tokyo. Draeger (1973: 85) says he was born in Sagami-han (now Kanagawa-ken). The sword drawing art he developed was named the Shinmei Muso-ryu Battojutsu (Muso-ryu) or Jushin-ryu, *Jushin* being an alternative *kanji* reading for Shigenobu. Shigenobu has consequently been given the title of the first headmaster of both the Muso Jikiden Eishin-ryu and the Muso Shinden-ryu. Some of Shigenobu's students went on to found such traditions as the Hoki-ryu, the Tamiya-ryu, and the Sekiguchi-ryu.

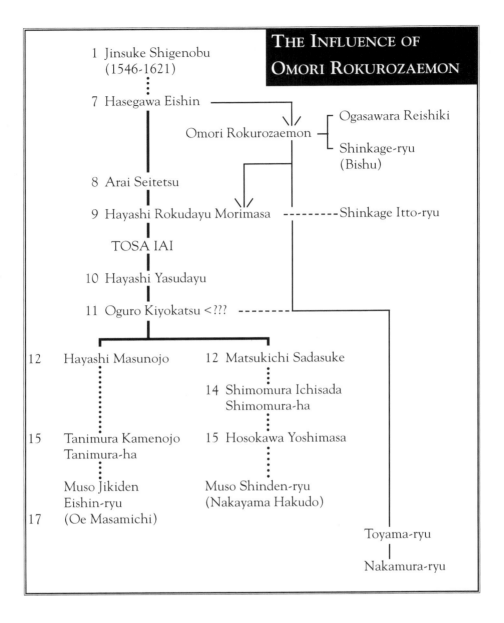

THE INFLUENCE OF
OMORI ROKUROZAEMON

1 Jinsuke Shigenobu
(1546-1621)

7 Hasegawa Eishin

Omori Rokurozaemon ── ┌ Ogasawara Reishiki
└ Shinkage-ryu
(Bishu)

8 Arai Seitetsu

9 Hayashi Rokudayu Morimasa ──────Shinkage Itto-ryu

TOSA IAI

10 Hayashi Yasudayu

11 Oguro Kiyokatsu <???

12 Hayashi Masunojo   12 Matsukichi Sadasuke

                            14 Shimomura Ichisada
                               Shimomura-ha

15 Tanimura Kamenojo   15 Hosokawa Yoshimasa
   Tanimura-ha

   Muso Jikiden   Muso Shinden-ryu
   Eishin-ryu   (Nakayama Hakudo)
17 (Oe Masamichi)

                                        Toyama-ryu

                                        Nakamura-ryu

Hasegawa Chikara-no-suke Eishin (or Hidenobu, an alternate reading of the kanji for Eishin) became the seventh headmaster of Shinmei Muso-ryu in 1610 (Jones, 1989). Eishin transformed many of the techniques and is said to have devised the style of drawing with the blade edge up in the sash. He added seated techniques (called *chuden* in Muso Shinden-ryu and *tatehiza* in Muso Jikiden Eishin-ryu) to the "secret iai" (*oku iai*) levels of technique. The *tatehiza* techniques are done from a position with the left knee on the ground and the right knee raised. The *oku* iai techniques are also done from *tatehiza* and from a standing position.

Eishin may have first used the name Muso Jikiden, although the use of the name Muso Jikiden Eishin-ryu can be attributed to Oe Masamichi Shikei (1852-1927) around 1918. It is more likely that the school was called the Muso Hasagawa Eishin-ryu in Eishin's time.

Omori Rokurozaemon Masamitsu was a student of Eishin's sword art and may have been expelled from the *ryu* by Eishin for personal reasons (Warner and Draeger, 1984: 89). Omori was a student of Ogasawara-ryu *reishiki* or etiquette as well as the Shinkage-ryu (Bishu) sword school. Today, the Owari Yagyu Shinkage-ryu has two sets of iai practice, the first of which starts from the formal seated posture called *seiza*. Rokurozaemon developed a set of eleven iai techniques that were initiated from the seiza and he was later re-admitted to the Muso Hasagawa Eishin-ryu. An old anonymous Japanese reference states that Omori took five kata from the Shinkage-ryu and five from Eishin-ryu, and then adapted these to fit the Ogasawara-ryu etiquette.

Hayashi Rokudayu Morimasa (1661-1732) of Kochi on Shikoku Island, the ninth headmaster of the Shinmei Muso-ryu lineage, was a retainer of Yamanouchi Toyomasa, the Tosa lord (*daimyo*). It is said that he was a head cook, but since he was a high ranking samurai, this likely means that he was more of a quartermaster than a chef, although amongst his many accomplishments, Hayashi was a master of *hocho jutsu* or the art of the kitchen knife. While in Edo, in attendance to Lord Yamanouchi, Hayashi studied the Shinkage Itto-ryu of the Mito Han (Warner and Draeger, 1982: 88). He was also a student of Arai Seitetsu Kiyonobu, the eighth headmaster of the Muso Jikiden Eishin-ryu. There are several skills that Hayashi was said to have mastered and he was, in fact, quite a renaissance man.

Arai was the last headmaster from the Tokyo area. After him, the lineage shifted to Tosa where the ryu became "secret," limited to those from Kochi with no "outsiders" allowed to study. The "secret teaching" continued on through to the seventeenth headmaster, Oe Masamichi, at which point it became widespread again (Jones, 1994).

Hayashi studied Shinkage-ryu kenjutsu with Omori Masamitsu and learned the Omori-ryu iai. On his return to Tosa, Hayashi taught the katas from the Muso-ryu/Eishin-ryu lineage and also incorporated Omori-ryu seiza iai. Up to this point, the Muso-ryu had only contained techniques that began from the *tatehiza* (right knee raised) and *tachi* (standing) positions. The seiza set became the initiation or *shoden* to iaido (*sho*, beginning; *den*, initiation).

Being a top samurai, Hayashi Morimasa had no need to open a fencing school when he returned to Tosa, but he taught his adopted son, Hayashi Yasudayu Seisho (d. 1776), who became the tenth headmaster. In turn, Hayashi Yasudayu taught Oguro Motoemon Kiyokatsu, who became the eleventh headmaster. Oguro is also said to have studied under Omori Masamitsu (Warner and Draeger, 1984: 89) but this is doubtful since Omori would have been very old and Oguro was in Tosa while Omori was a masterless warrior (*ronin*) in Edo. It is not impossible, however, since Oguro may have traveled to Edo with the Tosa lord.

Although Omori was never a headmaster in the Shinmei Muso-ryu lineage, he had a direct and vital influence on the school, being an instructor to one and possibly two headmasters. The relationship of Omori to Shinmei Muso-ryu is shown in the chart on page 72.

After Oguro, the school split into two lines, the Shimomura and the Tanimura. The Tanimura line is named for the fifteenth headmaster, Tanimura Kamenojo Yorikatsu (d. 1862), and is assumed to have been associated with the "common" folk (*goshi*, farmer/warriors); while the Shimomura line, named for the fourteenth headmaster, Shimomura Moichi Sadamasa, stayed closer to the samurai classes.

These samurai were members of the Yamanouchi clan, who were supporters of Tokugawa Ieyasu; while the men of the former rulers, the Choso-kabe, who had supported the Toyotomi against Tokugawa and were still too powerful to be eliminated, became the basis of the country gentry or *goshi*.

In the Taisho Era (1912-1926), the seventeenth headmaster of the Tanimura line, Oe Masamichi (1852-1927), reorganized Tosa iai and officially incorporated the Omori-ryu iai techniques as the beginning level. Oe is the man who named the school the Muso Jikiden Eishin-ryu and set its present three-level system using the Omori, Eishin, and Shinmei Muso-ryu kata.

Oe Masamichi practiced techniques of both the Shimomura and Tanimura lines. He was offered the Shimomura-ha headmaster position by the fifteenth headmaster of that line, Hosokawa Gisho Yoshimasa (c. 1848-1923), but refused it, subsequently becoming the seventeenth headmaster of the Tanimura line (Jones, 1994).

The true Shimomura line is considered to have ended with Hosokawa, and even the Tanimura line has not followed a true course since Oe Masamichi's time. The eighteenth headmaster of this line was Hokiyama Namio, who was a kendo teacher at a high school in Kochi. He died early and the headmaster position passed to a fellow iaido student, Fukui Harumasa, who was the judo teacher at the same school. If Hokiyama had lived longer, the headmaster course may well have been different. Fukui Harumasa was transferred to a school in Osaka, taking the headmaster position out of Kochi. Kono Hyakuren Minoru of Kumamoto (Kyushu Island) was working in Osaka and trained with Fukui Harumasa. He particularly wanted to be the twentieth headmaster, so the story goes that he "bought" the position. At this point, the headmaster position moved to Kyushu Island, but many people no longer recognize the lineage as being valid (Jones, 1994).

Nakayama Hakudo (1869-1958) of Tokyo studied under teachers from both branches of the Muso Jikiden Eishin-ryu and his teachings were later called the Muso Shinden-ryu. He adopted Oe Masamichi's three-level organization of the katas in his own teaching. The two schools teach similar techniques, the katas differing slightly in performance. The Muso Jikiden Eishin-ryu has eleven Omori-ryu techniques (and one common variation) while the Muso Shinden-ryu has added one more (the variation) for a total of twelve. The names used for the individual techniques are different for each school. It should be stressed that Muso Shinden-ryu and Muso Jikiden Eishin-ryu are, essentially, the same school. The katas may appear to be different but their "combative application" and the sequence in which they are taught are almost identical.

Other Schools Derived From Omori-ryu

The influence of the Omori-ryu was not confined to the Shinmei Muso-ryu lineage. It also played a somewhat paradoxical role in the emergence of the modern iaijutsu schools (Draeger, 1974: 65-67).

Toyama-ryu

In 1873, the Rikugun Toyama Gakko was set up as an army training school. The school included instruction in the sword and, in 1925, the Toyama-ryu *gunto soho* (army sword techniques) were defined. The *gunto* was the later army sword of katana design and mounted somewhat like the old *tachi*, suspended from the belt instead of tucked through it. Teaching at the Toyama Gakko were swordsmen skilled in the Omori-ryu.[2] These instructors developed a set of seven iaido techniques for the gunto that were performed from the standing position and were practiced with the aid of a belt with loops for the scabbard worn over the army trousers.[3]

This school was very much associated with the ultranationalistic right wing of the Imperial Japanese Army. The government used the sword arts and the other budo of this time to stir up patriotic and imperialistic feelings in the population.

Nakamura-ryu

Nakamura Taisaburo (b. 1911) studied the Toyama-ryu *gunto soho* and is one of the authorities on the school. He created the Nakamura-ryu and has defined battojutsu as its essential element. Nakamura eliminated the formal kneeling-sitting position saying that it is not practical. He also stresses the importance of sword testing practice (*tameshigiri*).

From the standing iaijutsu of Hayashizaki Shigenobu and Hasagawa Eishin; to the origin of Omori-ryu iaido as a school incorporating formal sitting (*seiza*) and etiquette (*reishiki*); to the modern iaijutsu of Nakamura, which rejects the formal sitting position, we seem to have come full circle.

Modern Omori-ryu Practice

The Omori-ryu as it is practiced in the Muso Jikiden Eishin-ryu is a highly formal set performed for the most part from formal sitting. Great stress is placed on precise physical and mental form. The set is as much about etiquette (*reishiki*) as it is about iaido, but since budo begins and ends with etiquette, this idea is not a problem for most students.

Why learn Omori-ryu first? What was the reasoning behind this choice instead of, perhaps, a set of standing techniques? It can be argued that the standing techniques are easier to learn and they are, after all, "practical." Anyone seeing them would not be tempted to say that iaido was less "combat real" than iaijutsu.

Figure 1a: *Tatehiza* (raised knee position). Note the right foot by the left knee. Demonstrated by Carole Galligan.

76

It probably is not hard to understand why the raised knee position (*tatehiza*) is not used as the starting point any more, as it may have been in Eishin's time (Fig. 1a). The pains in the left leg would just about guarantee that nobody would learn proper technique, simply because of the distraction. What should be resisted, however, is the temptation to say that, since the Japanese student was used to formal sitting, it was a good starting point because it was familiar. Standing is even more familiar and is the position from which the sword is most likely to be drawn.

Even if we accept Omori-ryu as the starting set and formal sitting as the starting position, why would Nakayama Hakudo and Oe Masamichi then choose the raised knee (*tatehiza*) techniques for the next level of technique? The very last techniques that are learned in the school, the standing techniques, are the "easiest."

But are the standing techniques really the easiest to learn? Surely the Muso-ryu headmasters from Hayashi Rokudayu onward had some reason for making Omori-ryu the beginning level. Let's assume they knew better than we and try to find some explanation.

First and perhaps most importantly, Omori-ryu introduces students to formal sitting (Fig. 1b). Perhaps no other martial art, including aikido, uses this position as extensively as does iaido. Seiza is a fundamental posture of the body, one of the few that is almost perfectly balanced and, as such, is a key meditation pose. Whole schools of therapy have been developed around this way of sitting, so it is not surprising that instructors would want to introduce it to their students early in their training.

Figure 1b:
The seiza position.

The most striking thing about Omori-ryu is that most of the cuts are done from a kneeling position. This does not allow the student to swing the sword too far down or it will hit the floor. It removes the need to teach the student not to finish the cuts too low. Without being shown or told, the student discovers *shibori* (wringing the hands inward) and *tenouchi* (pulling the sword up into the palm), or at least discovers the need for them. These are the subtle gripping techniques that allow the sword to be used properly. Kneeling also removes three out of seven joints from consideration while learning how to cut. The wisdom of this becomes apparent when you try to teach a student how to cut from a standing position. Tell a beginner to make a big cut keeping the hips low and the back straight; it will not happen.

Now put the student on one knee and ask for a big cut. The hips stay down since the toes, ankles, and knees are not available to push them up. The back stays straight since if it moves, the kneecap is likely to grind around on the floor. The hips stay square to the cut for the same reason. The student has only the shoulders and arms to swing with, allowing the instructor to concentrate on them.

The formal sitting position itself is useful. The scabbard must be properly controlled in the belt or the tip will hit the floor. The student's back can easily be kept straight since only the hip joint is involved in letting it bend. The draw and cut (*nuki tsuke*) is simplified with only one possible orientation of the hips. Spiritually, the student begins and finishes in the most humble position possible, one that is close to the floor. The position is vulnerable to attack and therefore cannot be aggressive as the raised knee or standing techniques. Moving up to a standing position from seiza requires great leg strength, giving the student a good root into the ground. Sitting solidly in seiza allows the student to know what that root should feel like while standing.

The list of benefits is long and if one considers all the instruction ever given in the iai arts, almost all of it can be examined in the Omori-ryu. Omori is initiation. It is the teaching set. It is the place where we learn to walk; later we run. Counting the partner practices, the Muso Jikiden Eishin-ryu contains somewhat over sixty katas. The average person could probably memorize that many movements in a month, so the object of iaido is not to see how many katas we can memorize. The object is to perform one technique perfectly at the proper moment. For that you need know only one technique, but you need to be able to do it properly. The argument is the old one of "quality vs. quantity." To do iaido, you must know how to cut, which Omori-ryu teaches. To do iaido, you must know how to carry your sword, which Omori-ryu teaches. Patience, perseverance, perspective, perception, perspiration, and all the other "p" words of practice (yes, even pain) are taught in Omori-ryu. It is *shoden* (initiation), as important as your first breath of air. Remember though, the set is not "beginner's stuff"; if an iaido practitioner could perform a perfect *mae* (first technique), he would achieve the perfection of iai. Malcolm Shewan (1983: 64) describes the kata as idealized and often impractical movements that are not meant to be battlefield maneuvers. Instead, they are a matrix within which we can relive the experience of the man who created the katas. Omori-ryu is a complete set and we should look at it as such, seeing the underlying principles of the whole and the intentions of the headmasters who have passed the katas along. We will attempt to discover some of those intentions after dealing with a few objections to iaido.

Objections to Iaido and the Relationship to Iaijutsu

As was mentioned earlier, the fact that the Muso Shinden/Jikiden teaching begins with Omori-ryu has often created the impression that iaido is something overly concerned with form and etiquette, having nothing to do with "real" iaijutsu. This is rather like watching someone hit a tennis ball against a wall and then saying the game is silly since the wall does not hit the ball back. Some of the comments on iaido published in English language sources over the last few years are typical of this attitude.

Otake Ritsuke (1977: 22) described modern iaido as having a sheathing (*noto*) that is too fast, saying that this is an affectation for show only and is dangerous. Iaijutsu instead emphasizes a fast draw and cut (*haya nuki*) that are more realistic and practical.

In fact, Omori-ryu has a slow sheathing, but also a slow draw and cut. Both are performed slowly to teach proper form. Iai from sitting and standing positions contain fast draws, but even here great speed is not attempted until the draw is smooth. Nakamura Taisaburo has several comments on iaido, claiming it is not practical or realistic. The comments are adapted from Draeger's *Martial Arts and Ways of Japan* (1974: 67-68).

1) Seiza was not a position the classical warrior would adopt. It is not a practical posture when one is armed with the daisho (paired long and short swords).

The classical warrior was more likely to be wearing a long, curved sword and a short sword (*tanto*) than the large and small (*daisho*) paired swords that did not become popular until the Edo period (1600-1868). The slightly curved "new sword" (*shinto*) or katana was not introduced until the middle 1500's and the paired style was developed much later (Sato, 1983: 61-62). The very warriors that would have carried and used the paired swords, the Tokugawa-era samurai, were those who developed and adopted the Omori-ryu.

Figure 2a (left): *Nuki tsuke* (raised knee position) showing
an opening for attack to the right wrist.
Figure 2b (right): *Nuki tsuke* showing the right wrist protected.

The iaido schools' upper levels do indeed begin from the "battlefield" positions, resting on one knee or standing and walking around. In point of fact, a soldier who has not yet drawn his weapon when he meets the enemy is not a soldier for long and iaijutsu would have no more use on a battlefield than iaido.

Obata Toshishiro was a student of Nakamura Taisaburo and has developed his own sword style in California. In his book, *Crimson Steel* (1987: 26), he states: "The samurai never wore his long sword when seated because it was not worn into the house, yet 'iaido' as the new sword drawing art was termed, taught many sword drawing methods from the formal seated 'seiza' position."

The samurai did indeed wear his long sword when seated. He wore it when he practiced Omori-ryu iai. At the time, the art might have been called *battojutsu*, *iaijutsu*, or some other name, since the term *iaido* did not become popular until the 1930's. The common people in the Edo period did not practice swordsmanship, therefore, the samurai most certainly practiced iaijutsu from the formal sitting posture.

Reid and Croucher (1983: 185) have this to say: "When it is well performed, *iai-do* is a beautiful, almost balletic use of the sword, but it bears little relation to the speed, poise and concentration of the art of iai-jutsu. The combat value of studying *iai-do*, especially with a blunt sword, is almost nil, but on the other hand the aim of the adept in this way is spiritual and bodily harmony and growth, not killing power."

If one needs killing power to have speed, poise, and concentration, perhaps one should practice with automatic rifles instead of these horridly inefficient blunt swords.

2) Iaido's nuki tsuke (sword draw) is too slow. It further exposes suki (a weakness).

This is doubtless true for the beginner practicing Omori-ryu, since a beginner is almost by definition exposing *suki* (an opening to attack) most of the time. This would not change whether a slow or a fast draw and cut was being attempted. Figure 2a shows the drawing motion performed with the right wrist exposed. Figure 2b shows the correct position of the hand with the sword's handle protecting the right wrist. For the expert, the draw can be slow or fast––the opening will not be there. As with most martial endeavors, speed is not as important as proper timing. If speed were all that was needed, the heavyweight boxing crown would be held by a flyweight.

The Muso Jikiden Eishin-ryu draw and cut can be very fast in the upper levels of practice. As we will point out later, there are important ethical reasons for teaching a slow draw and cut in Omori-ryu.

3) The iaido students' kiri tsuke (cutting action) is weak since they lack tameshigiri experience.

To our knowledge, there is no law that prohibits an iaido practitioner from using straw testing bundles while allowing iaijutsu practitioners to use them. Anyone can practice test cutting (*tameshigiri*). When you begin practicing, however, you have a better chance of making your cuts if you have been taught the proper mechanics of cutting. As was explained earlier, a great way to learn this is by practicing Omori-ryu. The Muso-ryu *iai-giri-do*, which was developed from the Muso Jikiden Eishin-ryu and which is still associated with this school, uses the Omori-ryu kata in combination with cutting practice as its first level of instruction. This is a rather intimate connection between iaido and cutting practice.

> 4) Iaido chiburi ("shake off blood") is not practical. Only by wiping the blade on a cloth or a piece of paper would the blade be clean enough to return to the scabbard.

This is true. The Tenshin Shoden Katori Shinto-ryu iaijutsu has a *chiburi* that consists of spinning the blade and then hitting the handle with a fist. The Toyama-ryu iaijutsu uses the exact same circular *chiburi* as does Omori-ryu. The *chiburi* "represented" by these motions would not be performed by a swordsman after actually cutting someone or something. An iaido exponent would doubtless use a cloth too.

> 5) The iaido noto of is too fast and is used only for show; the classical warrior's noto of is slow and demonstrates zanshin (lingering heart, awareness).

The iaido student had better demonstrate vigilance and alertness (*zanshin*) or the instructor will soon show their usefulness. As to the quick sheathing, it might be argued that one should be ready for further attacks after finishing one opponent. By taking a long time to replace the sword in its scabbard, you are leaving an opening of the same sort that is left with a slow draw and cut. In any case, fast or slow, drawing or sheathing, you must be ready to change according to the circumstances reflecting an "immovable mind" (*fudo-shin*). In fact, the sheathing of Omori-ryu is very slow, especially if compared to advanced level practice.

> 6) Modern iaido students' manners and customs are careless. Most have a koiguchi (open end of the scabbard) that is chipped and scratched.

All beginners have a scabbard that is chiseled. Nobody starts out with perfect technique. Omori-ryu is a school that contains major influences from Ogasawara-ryu etiquette. Omori-ryu is a school of the manners and customs of the sword. A poor student of Omori-ryu will have poor manners, but that is no fault of iaido itself. To demonstrate the type of etiquette learned in this school, several of the bows are described in the following paragraphs.

As students arrive for class, they are expected to carry the sword in a precise manner and to keep their arms and legs under control. Upon entering and when greeting or thanking a partner during class, a small standing bow of about ten to fifteen degrees is made (Fig. 3a). The sword is kept in the left hand, or in the belt if bowing during a class. The second bow is a more formal one to the high point in the room (Fig. 3b). For this bow, the sword is transferred to the right hand, with the edge facing back and the tip facing down in front of the students. The sword held in this way cannot be drawn easily or quickly.

Figure 3a: Standing bow on entry to the practice floor.

Figure 3b: Formal standing bow to high point in the room.

The bow is to about forty-five degrees and the eyes are dropped with the bow. Seated bows are also taught. In a formal seated bow (Fig. 3c), the blade is placed on the right-hand side with the blade edge facing the iaido practitioner. The handguard is lined up with the knee so that the sword does not stick out too far in front or back. The *hakama* is carefully moved out of the way so that the sword does not fly across the room if the student stands up quickly. The sword cannot be drawn easily from this position. The bow is performed in a precise manner with the hands placed carefully together in front and the back and head lowered until they are exactly parallel with the floor. Again, the eyes are lowered. There is no feeling of knocking the forehead on the floor and no feeling of watching your enemy in this bow; however, the hands are placed so as to pad the face should the head be suddenly shoved to the floor.

Figure 3c: Formal seated bow, to the instructor or the high point in the room. Note straight line of back and cupped position of hands.

Figure 3d: Seated bow to sword.
Note how difficult it would be to draw the sword.

When bowing to the sword (Fig. 3d), equal care is taken with its position. The bow illustrated here shows the blade resting with the handle to the left and the edge facing the iaido practitioner, again in a position that does not allow the sword to be drawn easily. This positioning of the sword and the depth of the bows are an essential part of etiquette. By your bows you can declare that you trust the person you are bowing to, that you are being careful, that they should watch out, that you respect them, or that you do not respect them. All of this and much more—from how to walk to how to sit—is taught in Omori-ryu. This attention to detail does not suggest that iaido students are ill-mannered at all.

The Meaning of the Omori-ryu Set

Let us now attempt to discover what the originators of the Omori-ryu meant their students to learn by doing these katas. We will examine the Muso Jikiden Eishin-ryu katas, although the lessons apply equally well to the Muso Shinden-ryu. There are several levels of instruction that are used to teach iai as students are led through the set of techniques over and over during their career. The katas themselves also introduce different concepts at each level as they are taught. The instructor will use a different approach for each student, depending on his or her skill.

The teaching "big, strong, fast, smooth" (*dai kyo soku kei*) is an indication of how students should be taught if they are to become good swordsmen. Too many students end up performing "sword-dance" by concentrating on the wrong things first—making pretty, flowing motions that would have no practical effect if cutting was intended. Another overall concept of instruction is "keep, break, leave" (*shu ha ri*). This indicates how each student should learn. Students begin by memorizing the movements and teachings of the instructor without question ("keep"). Only after they can mimic the instructor and they know the "shape" of the kata should the students demand to know the reasons for each of the movements ("break," as in "break down the meanings"). Finally, after the student can perform the movements with an understanding of each of them, the student must "leave" to study on his own and hopefully to improve the art.

We will examine a few of the mental and physical concepts included in the Omori-ryu katas. Some of these concepts are quite basic and would be taught to beginners. Others are more advanced. They are described here simply to illustrate the idea that a set of iai katas should be considered as a whole, and not an assembly of techniques thrown together.

The first kata is called *Mae* ("Front") and it breaks down precisely into the four main parts of an iai kata. The first movement is called *nuki tsuke* and consists of the draw and one-handed horizontal cut. Figure 4a illustrates the target of this cut. Of course, iai is not done with an actual opponent. These photographs are to illustrate a point. Those who advocate iaijutsu argue that this movement should not be performed slowly. In iaido, this move is performed with what is called "slow, faster, fastest" (*jo ha kyu*). The slow speed with which this kata begins has two purposes. The first is that one's hands come onto the sword handle so slowly and naturally that no outside observer can tell when they started moving and when the sword began to be drawn. The draw slowly accelerates while the defender gives the attacker time to back down. All through the draw until the tip of the sword is at the opening of the scabbard, the iaidoka is prepared to put the sword away and sit down again. During this movement, the iaidoka seeks to dominate and control the attacker's movements. It is only at the release of the tip from the scabbard that the "point of no return" is reached and the cut is made with full commitment. After this, there is no turning back and the motion is unstoppable. In learning this, we see that iaido is not intended to be an art of sudden attack or ambush, but one that seeks to control and avoid bloodshed. It is an art that intends to "win in the scabbard" (*saya no uchi no kachi*). Compare this to a sudden draw that gives an opponent no chance to change his mind, but simply cuts him down as quickly as possible. Figure 4b shows a common mistake made during the draw. Carole Galligan is leaning forward in an attempt to apply pressure (*seme*), but she is off-balance and not rising from her hips. Figure 4c shows the correct body posture.

Mae — the first kata in Omori-ryu. **Figure 4a:** The initial movement (*nuki tsuke*) of the first kata. The object is to cut across the shoulders.

Figure 4b-c: A common mistake in the draw is leaning foward (4b). Instead, the draw should be made while moving from the *hara* or stomach (4c).

The second part of the kata is called *kiri tsuke*. It is the finishing cut (Fig. 4d). Muso Jikiden Eishin-ryu uses a very large swing, starting with the tip of the sword behind the head at about shoulder height. To move into this position and then cut, students are taught how to apply both physical and mental pressure (*seme*) toward the attacker so as not to leave an opening for the attacker. This involves the principles of action and calm (*sei* and *do*) in combination. When the body is calm, the spirit is active and when the body is active, the spirit must be calm. Figure 4e shows a position that does not express *seme*. Bob MacMaster has created an opening by pulling his hands behind his head in an attempt to make a bigger cut. Figure 4f shows the proper hand position. In this photograph, the tip has been raised from its starting position, at the same height as MacMaster's neck, by using the left little finger.

Figure 4d: The finishing cut (*kiri tsuke*) from the first kata. Note the position of Galligan's hands and wrists as she extends the tip forward. The left foot is pushing her hips forward. **Figure 4e:** MacMaster demonstrates a swing that starts too far back, allowing for an attack to his head. His shoulders are also behind his center of gravity, which means he cannot more forward immediately.

Figure 4f: In this position shown, MacMaster's hands are in front of his forehead and he is still threatening his opponent. His shoulders are above his center so he can attack without preliminary adjustments.

The basic mechanics of cutting are taught at this point, and the kneeling position allows the instructor to concentrate on the arms. In the West, it is usually necessary to train students not to lead with their elbows as if they are throwing a baseball. This "whipping" action with the sword creates a very small cut that will not reach an opponent. The principles of proper grip are also taught here, so that the student does not cut into the floor.

Figure 4g shows the lack of a wringing motion in the wrists (*shibori*). The result is that when this cut is complete, the tip will hit the floor. Figure 4h shows the proper wrist position for this point in the swing.

Figure 4g: Chris Nunam is showing what happens with an incorrect *shibori*. Compare his wrist position to that shown in Figure 4-D. **Figure 4h:** By this time in the cut, the wrists should have returned to this position. The cut finishes with the top fo the guard at the same height as the top of the right knee.

The third section of the kata is called *chiburi* and symbolizes the cleaning of the blade in preparation for putting it away. The rather complicated circular motion that ends with the student standing up as the blade is "accelerated to a dead stop" relies on good leg strength and hip control. In figure 4i, Galligan's sword and left foot move quickly while her body moves up and forward slowly as one unit. She is watching the fallen opponent. The motions are extremely difficult to perform while maintaining *zanshin*, a feeling of lingering alertness that, in its original form, was designed to detect and prevent any further attack.

Figure 4i: Galligan is just finishing the *chiburi* movement of *Mae*. Note the stillness (*sei*) of her center and the activity (*do*) of the sword.

Finally, the blade is replaced in the scabbard while maintaining *zanshin* (Fig. 4j). The iaido practitioner never takes his eyes off of the attacker but the focus has now softened so that peripheral vision is being used. This soft focus or "looking at the far mountains" (*enzan no metsuke*) begins and ends each kata. The blade is replaced in such a way that it can be drawn again at any moment if need be. After putting the blade away and ensuring that no further attacks are coming, the iaido practitioner returns carefully to the starting position and only then relaxes the intense concentration and vigilance he has maintained throughout the exercise.

Figure 4j: The sheathing movement of the first kata. Even at this point, Galligan is ready to attack again. Note the right foot position as it supplies power to her hips.

This one kata could be used to teach almost every principle of iai, with no further techniques being needed. This of course is not really practical, and the longest even the most dedicated student can be expected to practice just one kata might be a year. The rest of the katas in the set are taught in sequence and several new concepts are introduced within each one. After watching several groups of beginners being taught and hearing the same topics introduced at the same point each time, the logic of the system is revealed and seniors begin to see that each kata is best suited to teaching a certain principle.

The second, third, and fourth kata are basically the first technique performed toward the left, the right, and the rear. During these katas, the student is taught how to turn on the knees, but more importantly, how to draw and cut accurately and without pause while turning toward an attacker. While doing these three katas, the student is also reinforcing the lessons learned from the first kata. The second kata is called *Migi*, or "Right," and the name refers to the direction faced before sitting down. Figure 5 shows the draw being made as MacMaster turns left toward Galligan. The attacker comes from the left side. The third kata is called *Hidari*, which means "Left" (Fig. 6, the attack is from the right); the fourth is called *Ushiro*, which means "Rear," and refers to both the direction faced before sitting and the direction of the attack (Fig. 7a). In figure 7b, note how the body is still providing a stable base from which to cut while the right hand and foot move into position. The student now has some tools to answer his question, "what if I am attacked from another direction?"

Migi, Hidari, & Ushiro

Figure 5: The draw and cut (*nuki tsuke*) movement of the second kata (*migi*). MacMaster is turning to his left, raising his left knee as he draws toward Galligan.

Figure 6: The draw and cut movement of the third kata (*hidari*). MacMaster has turned toward Galligan and is now simply doing *Mae* once more.

Figure 7a: The draw and cut movement of the fourth kata (*ushiro*). MacMaster has just begun to turn his body using his right knee and left foot, but he is already looking at Galligan.

Figure 7b: The completion of this move just as the sword is about to cut across. Taylor's body is moving from the hips toward the opponent.

The fifth kata is designed to answer the question, "what if my first cut misses?" *Yae Gaki* literally means "Eight Hedgerows" but refers to the thickets grown around castles for defense, so symbolically could mean "infinite defense" or "defense in depth." In this kata, the iaido practitioner begins exactly as for Mae, but the first horizontal cut fails to connect (Fig. 8a). The student immediately stands, takes a step toward the scrambling attacker and then cuts down vertically (Fig. 8b). At this point, the principle of "always being ready for anything" (*tsune ni itte kyu ni awasu*, or *i ai* for short) is demonstrated. The student is taught to cut as if the first motion will connect with the attacker, but not to rely on it connecting—to be prepared to move again. Students are often taught to push their left knee up off the floor as soon as the horizontal cut misses and then to move after the attacker. This demonstrates the need to have the left foot planted and pushing the hips forward while doing *nuki tsuke*, and the students can apply this instruction to the first four katas the next time they do them. The step and cut downward is assumed to have cut the attacker and the practitioner performs a horizontal *chiburi* motion before sheathing. Again, the idea of being prepared comes into play as the attacker swings his sword at the iaido practitioner's right knee (Fig. 8c). The iaido practitioner rises and blocks this cut, then shifts forward again to cut through the attacker's lower back (Fig. 8d). The same *chiburi* and sheathing as was done in *Mae* are now performed to complete the kata. This technique is an embodiment of the teachings of *zanshin* and *seme*.

Yae Gaki: Pat Senson, left; Chris Nunan, right. **Figure 8a:** Nunan has swung at Pat Senson who has avoided the cut by stepping back with his right leg.

Figure 8b: As Senson swings back his left knee trying to get enough room to free his sword, Nunan steps forward and cuts down on his head. Nunan is dropping down and forward onto his left knee as he cuts.

Figure 8c: Senson is not done yet and swings at Nunan's knee. Nunan stands up and shifts back as he blocks this swing. Note that Nunan's left foot is still pressing his hips toward Senson.

Figure 8d: Nunan shifts forward again and cuts through Senson's lower back. This cut must finish close to the floor or the target will not be hit.

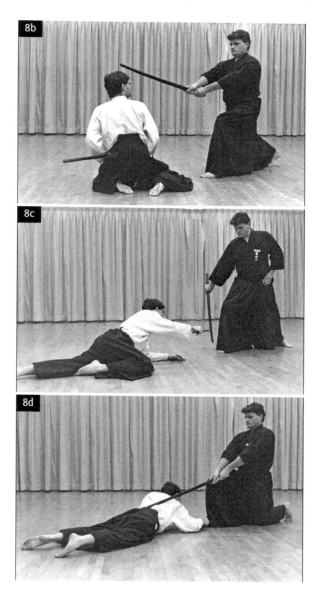

A variation of this kata has a second, standing attacker, approach from the front after the first vertical cut eliminates the first attacker. The block is transformed into another draw and horizontal cut, but the kata is otherwise largely the same as *Yae Gaki*.

The sixth kata is called *Uke Nagashi* ("Receive and Deflect"). It is designed to demonstrate how to handle an attack from a standing opponent who approaches suddenly from the left. There are several interpretations of this kata, depending on whether the attacker strikes once or twice and how soon you see him. If you see him in time, he will have only one swing. As the attacker approaches, the iaido practitioner draws the blade forward while looking left at the opponent (Fig. 9a). The blade is cleared from the scabbard and a deflecting block is made as the iaido practitioner rises up to a standing position (Fig. 9b). The right foot swings around so that the hips are lined up with the attacker and the blade is allowed to swing around after the block. The cut is made vertically down through the attacker's chest and it starts as a one-handed cut (Fig. 9c). As the blade hits the attacker, the left foot is stamped into a proper position. As the cut finishes, the right foot is brought up to the left and stamped down (Fig. 9d).

Uke Nagashi

Figure 9a: Nunan is now about to strike at Taylor's head.

Figure 9b: The strike is deflected as Taylor rises to a standing position.

Figure 9c: The blade is allowed to swing around after blocking and the right hand is used to start the cut. This photo shows Taylor about to cut into Nunan's left shoulder as he grasps the blade with the left hand to help the cut. Note that Nunan is unbalanced as a result of his missed cut.

Figure 9d: The right foot is brought up to the left as the cut is completed. The hips are well dropped. The back remains straight.

The movements to this point teach many valuable lessons about posture and about how the blade is held in the hand. An incorrect grip on the draw will result in the blade being knocked out of the right hand. A grip that is too stiff will not let the blade swing around properly and the one-handed cut cannot be made correctly (without pause), unless the principles of *tenouchi* (pulling the sword up into the palm) and *shibori* (wringing the hands inward) are understood. The back, hips, and legs must be correctly used or the body will not be in position to cut the attacker. It is in this kata that the principles of "mutual spacing" (*maai*) are usually introduced.

This kata's *chiburi* is called "blood wiping" (*chinagui)* and we should recall the complaint of Nakamura Taisaburo, who stated that the *chiburi* of iaido is unrealistic. In this case, the left foot is dropped back and the blade is placed across and just above the iaido practitioner's right knee (Fig. 9e). The right hand is now used to get a cloth and wipe the blade clean before the sword is returned to the scabbard. The cloth is not actually used during the kata but is only symbolically present (Fig. 9f). A reverse handed sheathing follows as the practitioner straightens his hips to face the front while still looking at the fallen opponent (Fig. 9g).

Figure 9-E: The blade is moved over the right knee as the left foot is dropped back. The right hand is reversed on the handle.

Figure 9-F: After an actual cut, a practitioner would use a cloth to clean the blade before putting it away.

Figure 9-G: After Taylor reverses his hand on the handle, the blade is swung around and placed into the scabbard as the hips are straightened and he drops down onto his left knee. Taylor is still looking at the fallen opponent.

The seventh kata that one learns in Omori-ryu, and therefore in the iaido teaching of this tradition, is *Kaeshaku*. The *kaeshaku* is the person who assists at a *seppuku* (suicide ritual, more vulgarly called *hara kiri*). It is interesting that immediately after the fundamentals of cutting are learned, the student is taught this kata. In a sense, it is quite logical that Kaeshaku is taught in Omori-ryu since the seppuku ritual is surrounded with elaborate etiquette and Omori-ryu is where etiquette is taught. Another, deeper meaning might be suggested, one that involves the seriousness with which students should take the study of iai. In this kata, the student draws the blade while taking a short step forward with the right foot, then stands, pulls that foot back and waits with the blade held in the right hand. During this movement, care is taken not to disturb the person performing seppuku. It is done quietly and smoothly. The rank of the person performing seppuku is reflected in what height the blade is held at this point. The higher the rank, the higher the sword. During practice, the middle level is always used (Figs. 10a-c). At the predetermined moment, the *Kaeshaku* cuts the neck of the person committing seppuku and severs the final bit of skin at the neck in the last movement of the cut (Fig. 10d) so that the head falls straight down rather than outward. The *Kaeshaku* then quietly performs *chinagui*, sheaths, and backs away from the body.

Students are taught never to demonstrate this kata, or to use it in competition. It is questionable whether it should even be illustrated in this chapter and it likely would not have been, except that it is such a vital part of the Omori-ryu set. By being a kata that does not involve an attacker, *Kaeshaku* does not involve any intimidation by mental or physical technique. This means that students should be able to feel a real difference between what they do in this kata and the rest of the katas in the set. If they do not feel any difference, it is a hint that they need to work on such things as *seme* in the other katas (or perhaps they need to learn how to relax in this one). At the moment of cutting, there must be an explosion of power to get through the spine cleanly with one stroke, especially since this is a one-handed cut. This is an opportunity to carefully study *kime* (focus), the concentration and explosion of power all at one time.

The next kata, *Tsuke Komi* ("Draw Close and Create an Opening"), begins to deal with the strategy of a sword fight, as well as the need to precisely control the "mutual spacing" (*maai*). As a standing attacker approaches, the iaido student draws forward almost as if to perform *Mae* (Fig. 11a). This move will slightly disrupt the attacker's timing and he will strike at the student's head. As he does this, the student stands up and pulls the right foot back while raising the blade overhead. The blade is raised in a "receive and deflect" position (*uke nagashi*) but there is no deflection. Instead, the attacker's blade misses down the front (Fig. 11b). Since the attacker was aiming at a kneeling target, his sword tip will now be low and the iaido practitioner can immediately cut down from the attacker's head to his chin (Fig. 11c). A second cut from head to groin follows (Fig. 11d) and the iaido practitioner steps back to cut a third time if necessary. The practitioner then sinks to one knee and performs another *chinagui* that represents wiping the blade with a cloth (Fig. 11e) or even with the *hakama* (Fig. 11f). The blade is then resheathed. This kata provides the opportunity to demonstrate that timing is much more important than speed. The student who simply rushes through the kata as quickly as possible will run himself onto the attacker's point. Of course, the student who waits too long or cannot move the blade correctly with the right hand, will not get the first cut in before the attacker raises his sword. Again, the student runs onto the point.

Tsuke Komi

Figure 11a: The initial movement of the eighth kata (*tsuke komi*), which causes the attacker to hesitate and cut a little sooner than he expected.

Figure 11b: Taylor rises up, guarding his head and allowing the cut to pass through where his body was in Figure 11a. **Figure 11c:** Starting the sword tip moving with the little finger of the right hand (see 11b), Taylor shifts forward and cuts Nunan down to the neck. Note that the feet are together and the hips are dropped. **Figure 11d:** Another shift forward to cut down to the waist. The feet are again together and the hips dropped even lower. **Figure 11e:** The *chinagui* of the eighth kata (*tsuke komi*). **Figure 11f:** This *chinagui*, using the hakama, is not actually performed when doing this kata.

The ninth kata is called *Tsuki Kage* ("Moon Shadow"). It is quite similar to *Uke Nagashi*, with a standing attacker approaching from the right side instead of the left. In this case, a block is not attempted. Instead, the iaido student draws and cuts the attacker's wrists (Fig. 12a). This kata's movements are similar to those in *Hidari*. In fact, if the attacker is close to connecting with his swing, the defender will simply perform *Hidari* and cut across his stomach under the swing (Fig. 12b). This kata allows the student to practice cutting the left (Fig. 12c), right (Fig. 12d), or both wrists by using different angles of draw. A partner can call out the target and the student must respond correctly. This develops a flexible attitude toward the kata. The usual method that is practiced is to cut both wrists (Fig. 12a). After cutting the wrists, the iaido practitioner shifts forward and cuts down vertically, finishing like *Hidari* but not dropping down onto one knee. Again, this kata is quite similar to *Hidari* or *Mae* and is simply applied to a different situation with appropriate modifications.

Tsuki Kage

Figure 12a: The draw and cut of *Tsuki Kage*. Galligan is cutting across and through both wrists. **Figure 12b:** If Galligan is slow to respond (note MacMaster's sword position), she must settle for cutting across MacMaster's stomach. **Figure 12c:** In this variation, Galligan is cutting upward through MacMaster's left wrist. **Figure 12d:** In another variation, Galligan is cutting downward through MacMaster's right wrist.

The tenth kata, *Oi Kaze* ("Chasing the Wind"), is the only one in Omori-ryu that begins from a standing position. In this case, the practitioner takes the initiative and forces the attacker to "pedal-back" while trying to draw his blade. The student pursues and when he sees that it cannot be avoided, he draws and cuts in the same way as was done in *Mae*. In Figure 13, Nunan is drawing his sword as he chases the opponent. Notice how his foot is placed onto the floor as he runs. This prevents him from tripping over his hakama. The kata, then, is simply *Mae* done while running forward.

Oi Kaze

Figure 13: The draw and cut of *Oi Kaze*. The sword is drawn while running, the toes are kept close to the floor to avoid catching the edge of the *hakama*.

This kata allows all the technical details learned in *Mae* to be practiced while standing. New concepts such as how to run safely while wearing a hakama and how to use the feet and hips to support a strong cut are introduced.

The final technique is "draw and cut" (*nuki uchi*), which illustrates the purest form of iai. The attacker is seated very close to the iaido practitioner who is forced to draw slightly off to the right side. The blade is raised overhead as the student comes up onto his toes and knees into the position called *kiza*. Without any pause, the blade is brought into position and a vertical cut is made while dropping the hips down and forward to create striking power.

Figure 14 shows Galligan cutting downward. Note the stable hips and shoulders as she uses the muscles of the chest and back to power the swing. A horizontal *chiburi* and sheathing follow without moving off of the knees, which are then brought back together and the student sits in seiza once more. This kata is the ultimate test of the correct application of handgrip and hip control. Even the sheathing is a test of the student's ability to know where his equipment is, since the end of the scabbard will usually hit the floor if he is careless. This kata teaches the student that what he might at first think is easy (just draw the sword, cut down, and put it away) is often quite difficult.

Figure 14: The draw and cut of *nuki uchi*. As the sword is cutting into the opponent, Galligan starts to drop her hips by pushing her knees forward and outward.

This chapter can cover only a few of the points that can and indeed must be taught to those studying the Omori-ryu, but even these few would require several years to fully understand. Iai is much more than the memorization of a few fast "moves."

We hope that the reader now has an appreciation for how closely the Omori-ryu has been associated with the Tosa school of Muso Jikiden Eishin-ryu, and how it may now be considered as a set within the school. We wish that by providing this brief history and explanation of Omori-ryu we have clarified its place in Japanese swordsmanship and answered some of the more common criticisms of iaido.

Note

1 The All-Japan Kendo Federation (*Zen Nihon Kendo Renmei*, ZNKR) has a set of iaido techniques (now called the *Zen Ken Ren Iai*) that have traditionally been called the *Seitei Gata Iai*. This is translated roughly as "representative techniques of iai." The All-Japan Iaido Federation (*Zen Nihon Iaido Ren-mei*, ZNIR) uses a common set called *Toho* or "sword art/way." In neither case are these sets called a "ryu." They are not a traditional lineage but are instead a grouping of techniques taken and, in many cases, modified from several traditions on the advice of a committee.

2 The Omori-ryu would have been part of Tosa iai at this time, but Oe's reforms would not have been fully implemented yet. As a result, Omori-ryu would often have been treated as a separate school, with Eishin-ryu and Shin-mei Muso-ryu being other schools all loosely associated and taught together.

3 Photos showing this belt may be seen in Obata (1986).

References

Draeger, D. (1973). *Classical budo–The martial arts and ways of Japan, vol. 2.* New York: Weatherhill.

Draeger, D. (1974). *Modern bujutsu and budo–The martial arts and ways of Japan, vol. 3.* New York: Weatherhill.

Jones, T. (April 1989). A brief history of iaido. *Kendo News, 4,* British Kendo Association, p. 4-5.

Jones, T. (1994). Personal communication.

Mears, B. (1990). *Yugen kan dojo iaido manual.* Fort Erie: Yugenkan.

Obata, T. (1986). *Naked blade.* Thousand Oaks, CA: Dragon Books.

Obata, T. (1987). *Chrimson steel.* Thousand Oaks, CA: Dragon Books.

Otake, R. (1977). *The deity and the sword, vol. 1.* Tokyo: Minato Research and Publication Co.

Reid, H. and Croucher, M. (1983). *The way of the warrior.* Toronto: Methuen.

Sato, K. (1983). *The Japanese sword.* Tokyo: Kodansha International.

Shewan, M. Tiki. (1983). *Iai: The art of Japanese swordsmanship.* Cannes: European Iaido Federation publication.

Taylor, K. (1993). The history of iaido–a Japanese sword art. *Journal of Asian Martial Arts, 2*(3): 36-63.

Warner, G. and Draeger, D. (1982). *Japanese swordsmanship.* New York: Weatherhill.

6

Kindred Spirits
The Art of the Sword in Germany and Japan
by S. Matthew Galas, Esq.

In the foreground, a swordsman defends against his opponent's *Oberhau* (downwards cut) by striking his arm. To the left, another swordsman parries a similar attack with a *Zwerchhau* (horizontal cut). This cut simultaneously deflects the incoming blade and strikes the opponent's head. *All illustrations courtesy of S. M. Galas.*

Background

Historians and anthropologists have long recognized the many similarities between the cultures of feudal Japan and medieval Europe. The government by a feudal hierarchy based on military service, the domination of the battlefield by an elite warrior class with a strict code of conduct, the cultivation of arts and letters alongside the use of weapons—all of these subjects have been noted and discussed at length. Less attention, however, has been paid to the close parallels between the fighting arts of the European knight and the samurai of feudal Japan. This chapter will examine the art of the sword in medieval Germany, comparing and contrasting it with the classical Japanese martial traditions (*ryuha*). The period covered by this inquiry will reach from approximately 1350 until 1600. For the sake of brevity, the focus will be on general principles and combat philosophy rather than on specific techniques.

The student of the Japanese tradition is fortunate, since the martial arts of the classical warrior (*bushi*) have been handed down to the present as a living art. As a result, he need only look to surviving sword fighting schools (*kenjutsu*) for illumination. Despite this advantage, changes in the form of the Japanese sword, as well as the incremental modification of techniques by successive headmasters, make it difficult to determine whether the kenjutsu of today is truly the same as that practiced by the warriors of medieval Japan.

The European tradition presents even greater difficulty. The martial systems of medieval Europe are long dead, victims of the invention of gunpowder and firearms. Modern fencing offers no clues, derived as it is from the featherweight gentleman's sword of the 18th century. Further hindering this study is a host of stereotypes and misconceptions concerning the knight's armor and weapons.

Fortunately, these European arts are not lost, but merely forgotten. Although their existence has gone largely unnoticed, a whole series of medieval treatises on the art of the sword has survived to the present day. Approximately sixty in number, these *Fechtbuecher* (fencing manuals) contain the accumulated teachings of generations of German sword masters. The first of these manuals was written in 1389; the last of the series in 1612. The works of these German masters allow a detailed glimpse into the principles and techniques of what they called the *kunst des fechtens*—the art of fighting.

A Brief History

Nearly all of the surviving German manuals bear the mark of Johannes Liechtenauer, an influential sword master of the 14th century.[1] Liechtenauer travelled throughout Europe, studying under the finest swordsmen he could find. Returning to Germany, he systematized and perfected the lessons he had learned. Obsessed with secrecy, Liechtenauer consolidated his teachings into a series of verses so cryptic that only those initiated into their meaning could decipher them. Gathering a select group of students around him, the master taught his secrets to a chosen few.

After Liechtenauer's death, his disciples grew concerned about the growing corruption of the art by lesser masters. Dropping the veil of secrecy, they began writing manuals which interpreted the great master's verses and explained his rules of swordsmanship. For the next 250 years, German masters used these verses as a framework for teaching the art of the long sword.

During the 15th century, some of these masters enjoyed the patronage of the highest ranks of German nobility. Sigmund Ringeck taught swordsmanship to the powerful dukes of Bavaria, Ott the Jew served as wrestling master for the Hapsburg archdukes of Austria, while Hans Talhoffer tutored the nobility of Swabia. The prestige of these masters ensured the spread of Liechtenauer's teachings throughout Germany, Austria, and eastern Europe.

Aside from Johannes Liechtenauer, two other masters profoundly influenced the fighting arts of medieval Germany. The first of these was Ott the Jew, a wrestling master whose techniques were used to supplement the weapon arts. The second was Hans Lecküchner, a priest who adapted Liechtenauer's long sword techniques to suit the *messer*, a one-handed, machete-like weapon. The writings of both these masters were considered authoritative and were widely copied.[2]

Assisting the spread of Liechtenauer's teachings in the 15th century was the foundation of an influential, guild-like association of swordsmen known as the *Marxbrueder* (Brotherhood of Saint Mark). From their seat in the city of Frankfurt am Main, the Marxbrueder organized the teaching of the art and the licensing of new masters. Since many members of this organization were merchants, the practice of the *ritterliche kunst* (the knightly art) rapidly spread to the middle class.[3]

The advent of the printing press further assisted the dissemination of the art. The first printed book on the *kunst des fechtens* was published in Vienna, Austria, in 1516. This work proved so popular that it was even translated into French.[4] Thereafter, printed fencing manuals proliferated.

During the 16th century, the most prominent masters gravitated towards the great cities of Germany. Augsburg, Frankfurt, Nuremberg, and Strasbourg all were home to influential masters who published treatises on swordsmanship and the other martial arts. In 1570, the greatest of the later masters, Joachim Meyer, published an important manual in Strasbourg. This printed work was reprinted in 1600 and was widely distributed throughout Germany.

By the end of the 16th century, firearms had become so efficient that body armor was nearly useless. As the use of armor steadily declined, so too, did the need for a sword heavy enough to cope with it. In turn, the comparatively lightweight rapier became increasingly popular, eventually eclipsing the older, knightly weapon. The last manual of this series, published in 1612, devotes twice as much space to the rapier as it does to the long sword. Thereafter, fencing manuals tended to ignore the long sword, until it faded from the scene around the end of the 17th century.

In Japan, the oldest surviving school of swordsmanship is the Tenshin Shoden Katori Shinto-ryu.[5] Its founder, Iizasa Choisai Ienao (1387-1488), was born around the same time that Liechtenauer died in Germany. Choisai was one of a number of prominent Japanese swordsman who appeared in the 14th and 15th centuries. Like Johannes Liechtenauer, Choisai and his contemporaries were the product of chaotic social conditions and unceasing war, which brought about a flowering of the martial arts in both cultures.

However, this blossoming of swordsmanship took different paths in the two cultures. In Germany, Johannes Liechtenauer cast a shadow of influence that lasted well over two centuries. So great was his reputation that his teachings were almost universally adopted. Although a few masters varied from the mainstream in their interpretation of the great master's verses, there was essentially one unified system of swordsmanship throughout the German-speaking lands.

In contrast, Japan developed hundreds of competing schools, each with its own combat theory, philosophy, and techniques. Although the martial arts community outside of Japan tends to focus on Iizasa Choisai Ienao, he was merely one example of a much larger trend in Japanese society. The Katori Shrine, which his school is named after, was a flourishing center of martial training for decades before Choisai began his studies there. Other centers, such as the nearby Kashima Shrine, were just as important to the development of swordsmanship in Japan. Furthermore, other sword masters such as Tsukahara Bokuden, Hidetsuna Kamiizumi, and the Yagyu family played equally important roles in the development of kenjutsu. As a result, there is no single figure comparable to Johannes Liechtenauer who can be labeled as the father of Japanese swordsmanship.

In time, the introduction of firearms profoundly affected the martial arts of both countries. In the forward to his manual of 1570, Joachim Meyer attributes the decline in the art of the long sword to the widespread use of firearms, ". . . with which the most manly and valiant hero is sometimes robbed of his life . . . by the least and most cowardly."[6] The continuous wars of central Europe ensured that this trend continued, leading to the demise of the art.

In Japan, the introduction of firearms contributed instead to the survival of the sword-art. In 1575, a scant five years after Meyer voiced his complaint, General Oda Nobunaga's masses of harquebusiers won a crushing victory over classical bushi at the Battle of Nagashino. The decisive effect of the new weapon paved the way for the unification of Japan under the Tokugawa shogunate. Ironically, the peace brought about by the advent of the gun allowed the Japanese art of the long sword to survive and flourish—the opposite effect that it had in Europe.

The arrival of Dutch and Portuguese traders in the mid-16th century marked a period of contact and cultural exchange between the Japanese and the various countries of Europe. In particular, European military technology was a matter of keen interest to the Japanese. To what extent 16th century Japanese swordsmen studied European styles of fencing, however, is a matter of conjecture. Some have speculated that the various *Ni To* (two sword) styles which later flourished in Japan were inspired by the rapier and dagger fencing which was so popular among Spanish, Portuguese, and Dutch swordsmen of the time.

Any connection between European and Japanese long sword techniques is more tenuous still. The use of the long sword was rapidly declining in Europe during the late 16th and early 17th centuries. Instead, European fencing masters of the time devoted themselves to refining the use of the rapier; the long sword was increasingly dismissed as an anachronism. Although the long sword remained popular much longer in Germany than elsewhere in Europe, the number of German visitors to Japan during this period was insignificant.[7] Thus, the likelihood of any significant borrowing or exchange of long sword techniques appears minimal at best.

Techniques using quarterstaff and halbard,
from Joachim Meyer's manual of 1570.

An Overview of the German Sword Art

The German masters divided their techniques into three major categories: *Blossfechten* (unarmored combat), *Harnisch Fechten* (combat in armor), and *Rossfechten* (mounted combat). The most important weapon in each category was the long sword, since the principles of its use were considered applicable to all other weapons. Against unarmored foes, the long sword was used with both hands to cut, thrust, and parry. Against armored opponents, the swordsman grasped the middle of the blade with his left hand, while his right hand gripped the hilt. Held in this manner, the sword was used like a short spear, enabling forceful, accurate thrusts to be aimed at gaps in the opponent's armor. A third method was used when mounted; the swordsman wielded his sword in one hand, while managing the horse's reins with the other.

Liechtenauer's verses concentrate on the principal knightly weapons: the spear, the long sword, and the dagger. Later masters expanded this repertoire to include a variety of other weapons as well. Foremost among these were the machete-like *Messer*, the poleaxe or halbard, the staff, and the sword and buckler. The manuals cover each of these weapons in detail, including methods for disarming the opponent.

Alongside this arsenal of weapons, the German school placed a heavy emphasis on wrestling techniques. In addition to the usual techniques for dealing with an unarmed assailant, the manuals include detailed methods for neutralizing a knife-wielding opponent. Wrestling was fully integrated into weapons practice as well, with grappling and throwing techniques used at close quarters. Many works even describe techniques for wrestling on horseback, the object being to throw or drag the opponent from his mount.

The principal weapons of the classical bushi—*tachi, tanto, yari,* and *naginata*—are comparable in both form and function to the German long sword, dagger, spear, and poleaxe. Both cultures developed fencing systems for each of these weapons, including techniques for armored, unarmored, and (when applicable) mounted combat. Furthermore, both martial systems shared an emphasis on grappling techniques, whether armored or not. In a sense, both knights and samurai were generalists rather than specialists, since they were expected not only to be proficient in all weapons, but competent wrestlers as well.

One area where the two cultures differed was in their attitude towards archery. Although European knights were commonly taught to use both longbow and crossbow, they firmly believed that missile weapons were the domain of commoners. This disdain was best expressed by the author of one of the knightly epics: "A coward was he who first used the bow, for he feared to close with his enemy."[8] To the samurai, however, archery was a noble art, older and even more respected than the art of the sword.

Another difference is the inclusion of sword and buckler techniques in the German system. A buckler is a small, circular shield, perhaps a foot in diameter. The Japanese schools never seem to have emphasized this defensive weapon. Like their European counterparts, the Japanese bushi used large, standing shields to protect themselves against missile weapons, but for some reason they never adopted the shield in hand-to-hand combat.

The Development of the Long Sword

For centuries, the arms and armor of the European knight remained essentially unchanged. His armor consisted of chain mail and a shield; his weapons were a one-handed sword and a lance. A mounted warrior, the knight considered combat on foot the work of commoners. However, this status quo began to change in the late 13th century. The increasing use of crossbows and longbows—which could easily pierce chain mail—led to the development of heavier, more protective armor.[9] Furthermore, the appearance of disciplined bodies of infantry which could withstand a heavy cavalry charge forced the knight to fight some of his battles on foot.

These battlefield changes led to the development of a versatile new weapon, the long sword. Wielded with one hand on horseback, the long sword was used with two hands when fighting on foot. Generally measuring from four to four and a half feet in length, the new weapon was sturdy enough to cope with a fully armored opponent. However, its comparatively light weight of between three and four pounds made it useful against even unarmored foes.[10] Its straight, acutely-pointed, double-edged blade was equally well-adapted for cuting and thrusting. Wielded with one hand on horseback, the long sword had a long grip which allowed it to be used with two hands when fighting on foot.

First appearing in the 13th century, the long sword's versatility made it extremely popular with the knightly classes, both on the battlefield and off. In Germany, it became the principal knightly weapon until the abandonment of armor in the 17th century.[11]

Although the long sword is commonly thought of as a military weapon, contemporary artworks make clear that this weapon was also worn with civilian dress. Numerous paintings and woodcut prints depict men in civilian attire with long swords hanging at their sides or cradled under their arms. Thus, the long sword was not only an instrument of war, but was also used as a means of self-defense, both at home and on the street.

Like the long sword, the Japanese *katana* was an all-purpose weapon, designed for both one- and two-handed use, in both a military and civilian context. This unity of purpose resulted in startling parallels in technique between the German and Japanese schools of swordsmanship. For example, many of the stances used by these schools are identical. So are many of the basic cuts, thrusts, and parries. Furthermore, the styles of both nations have separate series of techniques specifically devised for armored and unarmored combat.

The most conspicuous difference between the two weapons is the curvature of the blade. The long sword has a straight blade, well-suited for thrusting. The katana's blade is curved, making for a more efficient cut.

A more significant difference between the two weapons is the number of edges. The long sword has a double-edged blade, while the katana is a single-edged weapon. As a result, German masters developed a variety of close-range attacks in which the back edge is used to make hooking cuts around an opponent's parry. The Japanese school lacks this series of techniques.

Fencing with the *düsack*, a single-edged blade with an integral guard. In the foreground, two stances. In the rear, grappling and trapping techniques. From Joachim Meyer's manual of 1570.

Another important difference is the length of the blade. The long sword's blade is approximately ten inches longer than that of the katana. This difference in length has a profound effect on technique once the swords are crossed. Since the katana has a shorter blade, it describes a shorter arc when cutting around to another target—resulting in greater speed. Conversely, the long German blade travels a longer arc when cutting to a new target—exposing the swordsman to the danger of a counterattack while he is in the midst of his cut. Thus, German sword techniques place a greater emphasis on maintaining blade contact once the swords have crossed, thrusting over or around the opponent's parry instead of cutting around to a new target. On the contrary, Japanese techniques seem to place more emphasis on leaving the opposing blade and striking around to a new target.

Finally, the two weapons are equipped with radically different styles of hilts. The long sword is equipped with a cross hilt, while the katana has a small, circular guard (*tsuba*). Compared to the minimalist tsuba, the long sword's cross hilt somewhat obstructs the free play of the wrists while cutting. However, the cross hilt allows a wide variety of parries and blade-trapping techniques that are impossible, or at least dangerous, with a tsuba.

Swordsmanship: Principles and Techniques

The remainder of this chapter will compare unarmored combat using the long sword with similar combat using the katana. For the sake of brevity, the focus will be on general principles and tendencies rather than on individual techniques. This comparison is made somewhat difficult by the sheer number of surviving Japanese *ryuha*, many of which have radically different combat philosophies. Another difficulty is the teaching method employed. The German masters used standard Western methodology, presenting general principles, and then applying them to individual techniques. The Japanese method takes the opposite approach, proceeding from the specific to the general. Thus, the underlying principles of Japanese swordsmanship are seldom made explicit. Instead, they must be deduced from the katas of the various ryuha.

Footwork

The German system considered proper coordination of hands and feet to be the foundation of good swordsmanship. When making a cut, a swordsman should always step forward with the foot on the same side that he is cutting from. Thus, if a swordsman intends to cut from the right side, he should initially position himself with his left foot forward. As he makes his cut, he should step forward with his right foot. The same applies when a swordsman desires to cut from the left; as he delivers the cut, he should step forward with his left foot. This cutting method allows the swordsman to put his body weight into the cut, while maintaining a balanced position. On the contrary, a swordsman who cuts from one side while stepping from the other places himself in a twisted, unbalanced position. This faulty cutting method also limits the range of his cut.

Other aspects of footwork include methods for sidestepping an opponent's attack, pivoting steps that enable a swordsman's attack to reach around an adversary's parry, and stepping patterns used to deceive an enemy.

The footwork used in the Japanese ryuha generally seems to conform to the same rule expressed by the German masters. Cuts from the right are usually made while stepping forward with the right foot, and vice versa. Most kenjutsu schools also make use of defensive footwork, such as sidesteps, to avoid an opponent's attack and diminish the force of his blow.

The Basic Cuts

According to Liechtenauer, only two basic types of cut can be made with the edge of the long sword. Cuts from above, travelling in a downward direction, are known as *Oberhau* (Over Cuts). Cuts made from below, travelling upward, are known as *Unterhau* (Under Cuts). Since these cuts can be delivered from either the right or left side, four basic cuts result. All other cuts are variations of these four basic cuts.[12]

Elaborating on the four cuts, the German masters taught their students to make cuts from eight directions. The downward cuts from either side can be made either vertically (*Scheitelhau*) or diagonally (*Zornhau*). Upward cuts can likewise be made either diagonally or vertically. Finally, cuts can also be made horizontally from either side (*Zwerchhau* or *Mittelhau*). Furthermore, each of these cuts can be made with either the front edge or the back edge of the blade. An eight-armed diagram, similar to an asterisk, was developed to illustrate the blade paths of these derivative cuts. Despite this complexity, the German masters emphasized that all of these techniques are simply variations of the four basic cuts mentioned above.

The cuts used in the Japanese ryuha are quite similar to those of the German school. The diagonal downward cuts (*kesa-giri* and *gyaku-kesa*) correspond closely to the *Zornhau* from right and left. Diagonal upward cuts from both sides, usually referred to as *kiri-age*, are common to kenjutsu as well. These are identical in form to the German *Unterhau*. Furthermore, some of the more modern Japanese schools teach cuts from eight directions, even using an eight-armed diagram similar to the German one mentioned above.

On the other hand, Japanese schools tend to place much greater emphasis on vertical downward cuts (*kiri-otoshi*) than the German system. This is especially the case in Itto-ryu and its derivative schools, from which modern kendo evolved.

Instruction in the use of the rapier. Note the diagram on the wall, which shows the eight directions from which cuts can be made. Nearby statues are marked with vertical, diagonal, and horizontal lines to show the targets for various cuts.

The Basic Thrusts

Despite the common misconception that thrusting techniques first appeared in the Renaissance, medieval sword masters fully appreciated the value of the thrust. Because of its speed and efficiency, the thrust was the preferred method for regaining the initiative after parrying an opponent's attack. In addition to the more typical thrusts along a straight line, the German manuals include techniques in which a cut is transformed into a thrust. The manuals refer to this variously as "throwing the point" or "making a thrust out of a cut."[13] This is accomplished by striking at the opponent's face or chest with the point of the sword, instead of the edge—like a coupè in modern fencing.

As with the cuts, the German manuals divide thrusting techniques into two categories: thrusts from above (*obere Ansetzen*) and thrusts from below (*untere Ansetzen*). Since each type of thrust can be made from either the right or the left, four basic thrusts result. Thrusts from above are usually made with the hands held high, with the blade sloping downward towards the opponent. Thrusts from below are generally made with the hands held low, the blade inclining upward towards the adversary. When thrusting from the right, the swordsman's wrists are crossed; when thrusting from the left, his wrists are uncrossed.

Finally, the German repertoire contains one-handed thrusts with the sword. Releasing the grip with his right hand, the swordsman steps forward with his left foot. As he does so, his left hand launches the point forward at the opponent's face or chest.

Nearly all of these techniques appear, with greater or lesser frequency, in the katas of the various Japanese ryuha. The only exception seems to be the cuts with the point, which are rendered difficult by the curve of the Japanese blade. As mentioned earlier, the main difference between the thrusting techniques of the two national systems is the emphasis placed upon them. This emphasis, in turn, seems based on the varying characteristics of Japanese and German blades.

The Four Lines of Attack

Liechtenauer divided the human body into four lines of attack, a division still used in modern fencing. He did this by drawing two imaginary lines through the body: one vertical, through the center line, the other horizontal, under the ribs. These lines divide the body into four quarters, each with particular techniques devised to attack it. At their most basic, these openings can be broken down into the right and left side of the head, and the right and left side of the body under the arms. In foot and mounted combat, however, variations exist in the number of openings.

The swordsman typically attacks the lower openings with an *Unterhau* (Under Cut). When attacking the upper openings, the swordsman uses either an *Oberhau* (Over Cut) or a *Zwerchhau* (Cross Cut), a horizontal blow. Of these two, the *Zwerchhau* is preferred, since the uplifted hilt provides better cover for the swordsman's head. Given a choice, a good swordsman always attacks the upper openings. Not only are these targets closer to him, but they are also harder to defend. In addition, a successful hit on the upper openings is far more likely to be lethal than a blow to the lower areas.

The Japanese schools lack a similar division of the body, concentrating instead on striking at the opponent's center. The targets of the basic cuts differ as well. For example, diagonal downward cuts such as *kesa-giri* are usually aimed at the juncture of the neck and shoulder, rather than the side of the head. Upward cuts (*kiriage*), however, are usually aimed at the sides of the body underneath the arms, much like the German *Unterhau*. Although no explicit teachings seem to exist in kenjutsu regarding the relative merit of cuts to the upper and lower body, the katas in most schools clearly favor cuts delivered at the upper body.[14]

The Stances

The German masters sternly warned against tarrying in the stances, since they believed a swordsman is better off attacking his opponent than lingering in a static position. One master observed that the stances are really nothing more than certain points in the course of an attack, at which the swordsman momentarily pauses to see whether he should continue with his current course of action or change course. This German disdain for tarrying in a stance is mirrored in the Japanese schools. In Yagyu Shinkage-ryu, for example, instructors emphasize that there are no *kamae* (stances), only *kurai*, which are explained as fleeting, momentary positions connected by techniques.

According to German theory, each stance has particular techniques best suited to it, as well as unique weaknesses. If he is familiar with the stances, a swordsman can predict his opponent's actions with a fair degree of certainty, simply based upon the way he holds his body and his sword. This concept is closely tied to the admonition against tarrying in a stance, since doing so makes the swordsman a ready mark. Japanese schools, too, espouse the belief that the respective postures of the swordsman and his opponent delimit the techniques that can be applied in a given encounter. This idea is often dramatized in the duels in samurai movies, in which the combatants circle one another, shifting from posture to posture.

Liechtenauer's verses advise the swordsman to use only four stances: *Ochs* (Ox), *Pflug* (Plow), *Alber* (Fool), and *vom Dach* (From the Roof). Each of these stances has a left and right side variation. Of these, the right side versions were considered the most important. Despite Liechtenauer's admonition to use only four stances, later masters developed a vast number of other positions. They justified this by classifying them as variations of the original four stances.

❶ *Ochs* (Ox): The Ochs is a high stance, best suited for delivering attacks from above. In this stance, the swordsman holds the weapon next to his head, with the point sloping down toward his opponent. This drooping blade position gives the stance its name, since it resembles the lowered horns of an ox. This stance appears in various kenjutsu ryuha; for example, Shinkage-ryu calls this stance *jokaku jun*.[15]

The right and left *Ochs* (Ox) stance, from a manual dating to around 1545. The blade positions are identical to those used in the *obere Ansetzen*, the thrusts from above. Both swordsman use blunt-edged, flat-tipped practice swords. The two Japanese stances are quite similar to the German *Ochs* stance. Taken from a 17th century version of the *Heiho Kaden Sho*.

❷ *Pflug* (Plow): The *Pflug* is a low stance which places the swordsman in an ideal position to cut or thrust upward at his opponent. The resulting pose roughly approximates the position taken when walking behind a plow, giving the stance its name. This stance appears in some Japanese schools as a variation of *chudan no kamae*.

Right: *Chudan no kamae*, similar in some respects to the left *Plug* stance. Unlike the German version, the Japanese stance has the arms extended forward, away from the body. Left: The left and right *Pflug* (Plow) stance. The wrists of the right-hand swordsman are crossed, although the illustration obscures this fact. These two blade positions are identical to those used in the *untere Ansetzen*, the thrusts from below.

117

❸ _Alber_ (Fool): This is a low stance which places the swordsman in an optimum position for defense. This stance takes its name from Liechtenauer's belief that only a fool stays on the defensive, relinquishing the initiative to his opponent. However, he acknowledged the superior defensive qualities of this stance by including it among his four. Other masters agreed, judging by another name for this stance—the _eiserne Pforte_ (Iron Gate). The _Alber_ stance is identical to the _gedan no kamae_ found in many Japanese schools.

The swordsman on the left is in the _Alber_ (Fool) stance. His opponent assumes the _vom Dach_ (From the Roof) stance. These positions are similar to the _gedan_ and _jodan no kamae_ commonly used in Japanese schools.

❹ _Vom Dach_ (From the Roof): Like the _Ochs_, this is a high stance, best suited for delivering cuts and thrusts from above. _Vom Dach_ is identical to the _jodan_ stance used in most Japanese schools.

The German and Japanese systems share other stances as well. For example, the German school contains stances identical to the Japanese _wakigamae_ and _basso no kamae_, to name but a few. The similarity between the two systems is more pronounced in the stances than in any other area. This is due in large part to simple body mechanics. Given a two-handed weapon, there are a limited number of positions in which the sword can be held.

Offensive and Defensive Principles

The most important lesson that Liechtenauer taught his students was the concept of _Vor_ (Before) and _Nach_ (After). By _Vor_, he meant the offensive principle; by _Nach_, the defensive principle. The importance he assigned to this lesson is reflected in the following verse:

Vor und Nach	'Before' and 'After'
die zway ding	these two things
sind aller kunst	are to all skill
ain ursprung	a well-spring

Vor (Before): According to Liechtenauer's teachings, a good swordsman always attacks first, seizing the initiative before his opponent has the chance. Whether this first attack hits or misses is irrelevant, since it forces the opponent to parry the blow. Regardless of the outcome of his first strike, the swordsman keeps attacking, showering blows on his opponent. This keeps the enemy on the defensive, merely reacting to the rain of attacks. Ideally, the opponent is kept so busy defending himself that he cannot launch any attacks of his own. Any pause in this onslaught is a cardinal error, since it grants the opponent an opportunity to seize the initiative and go on the offensive.

The swordsman should vary his attacks—cutting, thrusting, striking with the pommel of the sword, even closing in to wrestle with the opponent. Furthermore, a good swordsman varies his targets, sometimes striking high, other times low, sometimes to the left, sometimes to the right. This variety confuses the opponent and keeps him off balance, so that he never knows where the next attack will come from.

Nach (After): If the opponent attacks first, the swordsman is left with the *Nach*, or defensive principle. Liechtenauer taught that a swordsman who accepts this turn of events passively and merely parries his opponent's blows will eventually be struck and defeated. On the contrary, a good swordsman seeks to turn the tide by somehow regaining the initiative and going on the offensive.

The preferred method of regaining the initiative is by means of a counterattack. Ideally, the swordsman strikes in such a way that his sword deflects the incoming blow and hits the opponent at the same time. The most prized techniques in Liechtenauer's repertoire, known as the *Meisterhau* (Master Cuts), are largely designed to accomplish this goal. In the words of one master, "Beware of the parries, which only poor swordsmen use. And note: if your opponent cuts, you should cut, too; if he thrusts, you should thrust, too."[16]

Another method of regaining the initiative is for the swordsman to parry the incoming attack. The parry is always combined with a sidestep, which diminishes the power of the attack and robs the attacker of his proper distance.

After parrying, the swordsman immediately replies with an attack of his own before the opponent can strike again. However, since the attacker is already in motion, the German masters believed that it is easier for him to renew his attack than for the defender to riposte. Thus, they discouraged the use of parries, although they recognized that at times a swordsman has no choice.

In Japan, many kenjutsu schools use the concepts of *sen* (initiative) and *go* (response) to express similar ideas. *Sen* means to move before the opponent does, while *go* means allowing the enemy to move first. In addition to these relatively simple tactical concepts, some *ryuha* make use of more elaborate psychological constructs to analyze combat strategy. One example of this is the Shinkage family of *ryuha*, which place great importance on the concepts of *setsunin-to* (Killing Sword) and *katsujin-ken* (Life-Giving Sword). In techniques applying *setsunin-to*, the swordsman psychologically dominates and cows his opponent. The swordsman who uses *katsujin-ken*, on the other hand, lulls his opponent into a false sense of security, using his overconfidence as a tool to defeat him. In the schools descended from the Shinkage-ryu, the latter was considered far superior to the former.[17]

Attack and defense in one: although the swordsman on the left attacks first, his opponent steals the initiative from him by counterattacking with a cut underneath his blade. This cut will simultaneously parry the incoming blow and strike the opponent.

Both the tactical concepts and combat psychology of the Japanese schools overlap to some degree with the German principles of *Vor* and *Nach*. The concept of *Vor*, with its emphasis on striking first and dominating the opponent with incessant attacks, shares elements of both *sen* and *setsunin-to*. Despite the heavy bias against the *Nach*, or defensive principle, the German manuals list certain techniques in which the swordsman deliberately exposes himself, inviting his opponent to attack. These techniques are similar to Japanese methods using both the concepts of *go* and *katsujin-ken*.

As opposed to the German school, with its pronounced bias in favor of the offensive, the Japanese schools hold varying opinions of the relative merit of attack and defense. Some schools prefer to wait for the opponent to attack. Others agree with Liechtenauer, instructing their students to attack first. Similarly, some schools see killing the opponent—even at the cost of one's own life—as the principal goal. Others see self-defense—even if the opponent escapes unscathed—as the true object of swordsmanship.

The Use of Leverage

The German masters divided the blade of the sword into two parts, known as the *Stark* (Strong) and the *Schwech* (Weak). The *Stark* is the portion which reaches from the hilt up to the mid-point of the blade. Since this part of the blade is closest to the hands, it has the greatest leverage. Thus, the *Stark* is the defensive part of the sword, used for parrying an opponent's blows. The *Schwech* is the remainder of the blade, extending from the mid-section to the point of the sword. Since it is farthest from the hands, this part of the blade has the least amount of leverage. The *Schwech* is the offensive part of the blade, used for cutting and thrusting.

Whenever the blades cross, each combatant typically seeks to press his *Stark* against the *Schwech* of the opposing sword. By applying superior leverage, the swordsman gains control of his adversary's sword and clears an opening for attack. Mastery of this skill—the proper application of leverage—is extremely important in close combat, where the swords often come into contact.

In Japanese theory, the blade is usually divided into three parts: the *monouchi* (tip), the *chu-o* (middle) and the *tsuba moto* (closest to the guard). As in the German system, the *monouchi* is the offensive portion of the blade, while the *tsuba moto* is used to parry. In counterattacks, where the opponent's blade is deflected by the swordsman's cut, the *chu-o* is sometimes used to contact the opposing blade.

Although most Japanese schools tend to avoid the prolonged blade contact found in the German art, one ryu in particular specializes in techniques made with the swords crossed. Maniwa Nen-ryu places great emphasis on the proper use of leverage, training its students intensively in the engaged position known as *tsuba zerai*.[18]

Gauging the Opponent's Blade Pressure

Whenever a swordsman contacts his opponent's blade—with a cut, a thrust, a parry, or by simply crossing the opposing sword—he should immediately determine whether the pressure against his blade is *Hart* (Hard) or *Weich* (Soft). Hard pressure is when the opponent presses his sword forcefully against the opposing blade. Soft pressure is when the opponent places minimal pressure on the blade. This blade pressure plays a key role in determining which technique the swordsman would use next.

Liechtenauer taught that a good swordsman opposes weakness with strength, and strength with weakness. If an opponent's blade pressure is soft, the swordsman opposes this weakness with strength: remaining in contact with the blade, he applies the proper leverage to force it aside, attacking on the same side that his blade is already on. On the other hand, if the opponent's blade pressure is hard, pressing forcefully against the swordsman's blade, he opposes this strength with weakness: suddenly giving way, he releases his opponent's blade and cuts around to the other side.

According to the German manuals, the ability to properly gauge the opponent's blade pressure is the greatest skill in swordsmanship. If a swordsman correctly gauges the blade pressure and makes an appropriate response, the opponent will be struck before he is aware of what has happened. The 'soft' opponent will find his blade forced aside, without the leverage or distance required to parry the incoming attack. The 'hard' opponent will find his blade travelling swiftly in the wrong direction, away from the incoming cut or thrust that he needs to parry. The harder he presses, the further his blade moves when the pressure is released, and the more he exposes himself on the other side.

Some Japanese schools contain teachings which use a hard/soft dichotomy similar to that found in the German system. For example, Araki-ryu teaches its students *in-yo gaku*, the interplay of Yin and Yang. However, this school gives the hard/soft concept a much wider scope, applying it not only to physical technique, but also to tactical approaches and combat psychology.[19] Although other ryuha may lack an explicit expression of the concepts mentioned above, an understanding of these principles is implicit in many of their kata. Maniwa Nen-ryu, in particular, employs techniques in which the swordsman either forces his way through a weak engagement, or releases his opponent's hard pressure, cutting around to the other side. However, Japanese swordsmanship on the whole tends to avoid prolonged blade contact. As a result, these concepts are usually less important in the Japanese ryuha than they are in the German system.

Zufechten — The First Phase of Combat

The German masters divided combat into two phases. The *Zufechten* is the initial phase, in which the swordsman closes distance with his opponent. Starting out of striking distance, the swordsman assumes a stance and approaches his adversary. Stepping swiftly toward his opponent, the swordsman makes his first attack, usually a cut.

This first attack is usually made from the right side. When cutting from the right side, a swordsman's arms are uncrossed. Cuts from the left require him to cross his right wrist over the left. This latter position, with the wrists crossed, is weak, awkward, and unnatural. This is especially the case once the swords cross, and the application of leverage becomes important. As a result, the German masters preferred cuts made with the arms *offen* (open) as opposed to those in which the wrists are *krump* (crooked or twisted).

An inexperienced swordsman often fixates on his opponent's weapon, since it poses a threat to him. In the initial phase of combat, the novice often attempts to close distance by cutting at the opposing blade, seeking to beat it aside. Liechtenauer considered this a grave error. He believed that every action a swordsman makes should threaten the opponent, forcing him to parry unless he wants to be hit. In this way, the swordsman keeps the initiative and dictates his opponent's moves. Since the act of beating the blade aside poses no danger to the opponent, he is free to simply evade the attempt to strike his blade, taking the opportunity to attack. Thus, cutting at the opponent's sword instead of his body amounts to a voluntary relinquishment of the initiative—a cardinal sin in Liechtenauer's eyes. As one early master said, a good swordsman ". . . should act as if his opponent has no sword, or as if he doesn't see it. . . ."[20] Conversely, a swordsman should be skilled at evading the opponent's sword whenever he attempts to make contact, seizing the initiative and attacking the momentary opening that results.

Also belonging to the *Zufechten* phase are a variety of feints. Two primary methods are used. In the first, the swordsman simply pulls his blow before it lands, and then cuts or thrusts at another target. In the second method, the swordsman intentionally misses his opponent, cutting past him into another stance. From this new position, he makes his final attack at another opening. In both types, the feint begins as a real attack; the swordsman only evades the opposing blade when it appears likely that the opponent will parry the blow.

The concept of closing distance is central to most Japanese ryuha. They typically identify three types of encounters, based on the initial distance between the combatants: *yukiai* (going encounter), in which the combatants begin well out of range; *tachiai* (standing encounter), in which the combatants begin just out of range, with the sword tips barely crossed; and *iai* (seated encounter) in which one or more of the combatants is seated or kneeling. Mastery of the subtleties of *maai*, or combat distance, is considered especially important when using the sword against an unequal weapon—whether it be a tanto, yari, or naginata.

Although the Japanese schools lack an explicit teaching on the subject, their katas make clear that they share the German preference for making the first attack from the right. Cuts from the left, with the wrists crossed, are widely regarded as comparatively weak and awkward, and are generally avoided.

Krieg — The Second Phase of Combat

The realities of combat are such that a swordsman's initial attack is rarely successful. As a result, the combatants often find themselves facing each other at arms length, behind crossed swords. The manuals call this second phase of combat the *Krieg* (War), also known as *Handarbeit* (Hand-work). In this phase, the swordsman fight at close range, exchanging cuts, thrusts, and parries.[21]

During the *Krieg* phase, the swordsman showers his opponent with attacks. As soon as one is parried, he begins another. Since the blades are in such frequent contact, the swordsman must continually gauge his opponent's blade pressure, responding appropriately with 'soft' or 'hard' techniques. Meanwhile, the defending swordsman attempts to somehow regain the initiative, forcing the attacker onto the defensive.

Liechtenauer taught that whenever the blades cross, three main types of attack are possible: a thrust, a cut, and a *Schnitt* (Slice), a slicing or drawing cut. These three options are known as the *Drey Wunder* (Three Wounders). Knowing which of the three to use is an important skill in close combat. In large part, this choice is based on the swordsman's distance from his adversary: the thrust is a long range attack, the cut is used at medium range, and the *Schnitt* is most effective at close range. Choosing the wrong option is a potentially fatal mistake, since the swordsman must adjust his distance to compensate—losing valuable time in the process.

The techniques allocated to the *Krieg* phase can be broken down into two types. The first group of techniques, *vom Schwert* (from the sword), are made by leaving the opponent's blade. For example, if the opponent parries his cut, the swordsman removes his sword from contact with the opposing blade, striking at another opening. This new attack can be made as a cut, thrust, *Schnitt* (drawing cut), or even by striking with the pommel of the sword. These techniques are made with an absence of blade contact, aside from incidental contact resulting from an adversary's belated parry.

The second group of techniques are made *am Schwert* (on the sword). These are attacks made without leaving the opposing blade, maintaining constant blade contact throughout the course of the attack. Better known as the *Winden* (Winding or Turning), these techniques are one of the hallmarks of the *kunst des fechtens*. They typically involve the application of superior leverage against the opponent's blade. Pressing the *Stark* (Strong) of his blade against the opponent's *Schwech* (Weak), the swordsman clears an opening, while simultaneously sliding along the opposing blade to strike his head or torso. The name is derived from the winding, turning motion of the sword along its axis.

A *Winden*, an attack made while maintaining blade contact. The left-hand swordsman's initial attack, a *Scheitelhau* (vertical downward cut), has been parried. Remaining in contact with the opposing blade, he hooks over his opponent's parry with a back-edge cut to the head. This illustration comes from Albrecht Duerer's manual of 1512.

The *Winden* have two main advantages. First is the control they allow over the opposing blade, since the swordsman's blade never leaves his opponent's. Second is their speed, since the blade is already close to the opponent when the attack begins. Their only disadvantage is their relative lack of force. Although these *Zecken* or 'taps' with the sword are comparatively light, they often catch the opponent by surprise. This, in turn, often triggers an overreaction by the flustered opponent as he belatedly attempts to parry, creating an opportunity for the swordsman to deliver a killing blow to another target.

Another *Winden*, from Hans Talhoffer's manual of 1467. Originally, both swordsman were in the position assumed by the man on the left. The right-hand swordsman, sensing hard pressure on the blade, steps in with a thrust at his opponent. By uncrossing his arms, he can reach around the opposing blade with a thrust. The opponent's hard pressure causes his blade to follow, and prevents him from simply thrusting forward at his attacker's belly.

A similar division of combat into phases is found in Shinkage-ryu. According to a commentary on the *Heiho Kaden Sho*, the term *jo* refers to the period before the attack, *ha* to the initial attack, and *kyu* to the exchanging of blows that occurs after the first attack.[22] Thus, *jo* and *ha* correspond to the German *Zufechten*, while kyu seems to be the same as the *Krieg* or *Handarbeit* phase of combat.

Although both systems divide combat into similar phases, the methods used once the blades cross vary greatly. Techniques such as the *Winden*—cutting or thrusting without leaving the opponent's blade—appear with much less frequency in the Japanese schools. Although some schools, such as Maniwa Nen-ryu, do use these techniques, the general Japanese tendency is to avoid prolonged blade contact. One reason for this may be the length of the blades; since the German sword is longer, the swordsman are farther apart when the blades are crossed. This greater distance translates into greater reaction time for the swordsman. In comparison, the shorter Japanese blade places the combatants at much closer range when the blades are crossed. The swordsman are so close that they have much less time to react, making this engaged position far more dangerous.

Half-Sword Techniques

Another hallmark of the German school is a series of techniques in which the swordsman grasps the blade of the sword in his left hand, while holding the grip in his right. Holding the sword in this fashion, the swordsman uses it like a short spear to thrust at his opponent. The German masters referred to these as *Halb-Schwert* (Half-Sword) techniques. Designed primarily for use in armored combat, these methods were deemed so effective that many swordsman used them even when fighting unarmored. Although grasping a sharp blade would seem to create a risk of injury, the swordsman's hand was usually protected by a leather glove. These techniques were perfected by Master Martin Hundsfeld and Master Andre Liegnitzer, whose writings on the subject were widely copied.[23]

These Half-Sword techniques include ready stances, thrusts, pommel strikes, and parries—all with the left hand gripping the blade, Other moves include hooking and trapping maneuvers using the point, the pommel, or the cross hilt. With slight adjustments for the length of the weapon, these methods could easily be adapted for use with a spear or lance.

One of the most common Half-Sword techniques is the *Kron* (Crown) parry, used against a vertical downwards cut to the head. Holding the sword over his head with the point forward, the swordsman catches the incoming cut on the portion of the blade between his hands. This parry is typically followed by a thrust over the opponent's right arm at his face. In a more sophisticated version of this, the parry and thrust can be made as a single move, simultaneously blocking and striking the opponent.

Half-Sword—After parrying his opponent's thrust,
the swordsman reposts with a pommel strike.

Two Half-Sword stances, from Hans Talhoffer's manual of 1467. The swordsman on the left prepares to thrust from above; his opponent, from below.

A Japanese stance, similar in many respects to one of the stances in the preceding illustration.

Half-Sword techniques appear in some Japanese schools as well. Although most kenjutsu ryuha tend to avoid these methods, a few schools seem to specialize in them. Katori Shinto-ryu, in particular, contains a large number of these techniques in its katas.[24] For example, the *Kron* parry mentioned above is nearly identical to the *Tori* (Temple Gate) parry of this school. Other techniques involve cuts, thrusts and parries in which the blade is supported by the left hand. When using Half-Sword techniques, the Japanese swordsman typically pinches the blade between his thumb and forefinger, or rests the blunt back edge on the palm of his hand.

The main difference between the German and Japanese systems in this respect is the importance they ascribe to the techniques. In the Japanese system, these techniques are fairly uncommon, and appear to be a late development. Thus, they appear with greater frequency in the more recent iaido schools than they do in the older kenjutsu ryuha, with the exception of Katori Shinto-ryu. In contrast, Half-Sword techniques were a specialty of the German masters. In some of the surviving manuals, they comprise the majority of the repertoire. So common were these methods that artists depicted the German emperor himself using them on more than one occasion.[25]

Left: The swordsman on the left parries a downwards cut by sidestepping, hooking behind his opponent's blade, and guiding the cut past him. This type of redirecting parry was used against a strong opponent; against a weaker adversary, the swordsman would receive the cut on the portion of the blade between his hands.

Right: A similar Japanese parry, supporting the blade on the palm of the left hand. This type of parry is called *Tori* (Temple Gate) by the Katori Shinto-ryu. After receiving his opponent's cut, the swordsman thrusts over the opponent's arm at his face.

The greater popularity of these techniques in Germany is most likely due to the longer blade of the German sword. At close range, a technique that suddenly shortens the effective length of such a long blade is especially effective. In addition to allowing thrusts at extremely close range, these techniques give the swordsman much greater leverage than an opponent who uses a more conventional grip on the sword. In comparison, the Japanese blade is so short that only minimal advantage is gained by using such techniques.

Conclusion

In retrospect, it should not be surprising that two societies, each with a professional warrior class, should develop similar approaches to the martial arts. Considering the highly efficient armor used in both cultures, the focus on a two-handed weapon is also understandable. Given the mechanics of the human body, the similarity in ready stances and other basic elements of technique is only natural. The differences in technique which do exist are readily explained by the characteristics of the weapon itself, such as the length of blade or the number of edges.

Of course, certain aspects of both systems of swordsmanship are the result of cultural factors. For example, the emphasis on kata as a teaching method can be seen as part of a larger trend throughout all of the Japanese arts. Likewise, the spiritual emphasis so apparent in the Japanese martial tradition stems from the importance of esoteric forms of Buddhism, and later Zen, to the warrior class. Neither of these cultural factors existed in medieval Germany; thus, these elements are lacking in the *kunst des fechtens*. The German system, in turn, was influenced by larger intellectual currents in Europe. The first of the manuals, written by a German priest, even quotes Aristotle to support one of Liechtenauer's principles.[26] This close connection to the major sources of Western thought is reflected in the standard methodology used by German masters: beginning with general principles, they proceed to specific examples.

Finally, despite the misconceptions so rampant in the field, even a cursory study of the German manuals reveals a system of martial arts that was sophisticated, systematic, and highly effective. Far from an unskilled ruffian who relied on strength alone, the medieval knight is revealed in his true colors: a skilled professional, expert in his weapons, and possessed of a deadly repertoire of techniques—as effective, in every significant respect, as his counterparts in feudal Japan.

APPENDIX
The Primary Techniques with the Long Sword

Master Liechtenauer's verses list seventeen *Hauptstuecke* (Primary Techniques) used in unarmored combat with the long sword. First come the five *Meisterhau* (Master Cuts), a series of especially effective cuts made with the sword. They are followed by the remaining twelve techniques which Master Liechtenauer considered most useful in combat.

1) **Zornhau** (Rage Cut): A diagonal downwards cut which deflects the opponent's attack, while simultaneously striking him in the face with the point. This cut derives its name from Liechtenauer's recognition that a swordsman striking in anger will instinctively use this cut, which is a downward diagonal cut from the right shoulder.

2) **Krumphau** (Crooked Cut): A downwards cut, made with the back edge of the blade, which strikes the opponent's wrist. This technique is usually made while sidestepping to avoid the opponent's attack; the blow strikes the opponent's wrist, stopping his attack. The name is based on the *"krump"* (crooked or twisted) position of the swordsman's wrists, which are crossed in the process of making the blow.

3) **Zwerchhau** (Cross Cut): A horizontal cut which simultaneously deflects the opponent's attack and strikes him on the side of the head. The name derives from the horizontal trajectory of the blow.

4) **Schielhau** (Squinting Cut): A downwards cut, made with the back edge of the blade, which simultaneously deflects the opponent's attack and strikes him on the shoulder or neck. This cut is made with a pivoting sidestep. In the final position, the swordsman can only see his opponent out of one eye; hence the name.

5) **Schaitelhau** (Scalp Cut): A vertical downwards cut at the opponent's head, made with the very tip of the blade. The name is derived from the target of the attack.

6) **Vier Leger** (Four Stances): Described in the main body of this chapter, these are the Ox, Plow, Fool, and From the Roof.

7) **Vier Versetzen** (Four Counters): These are specific methods for attacking each of the four stances mentioned above. This series of verses also contains methods for dealing with an opponent who parries the swordsman's attack. The name comes from the specialized attacks which counter the defensive advantages of particular stances.

8) **Nachraissen** (Attacking After): Methods for regaining the initiative, should the opponent manage to attack first. These include dodging the opponent's attack, striking him while he is in the midst of his attack, and other methods. The name refers to the timing of the technique, since the swordsman allows his opponent to attack first before beginning his own *"raissen"* or attack.

9) **Ueberlauffen** (Overrunning): If the opponent strikes at the lower parts of the body, the swordsman is instructed to ignore the attack, instead striking at the upper parts of his adversary's body. Thus, he out reaches the opponent's attack.

10) **Absetzen** (Setting Aside): Methods for parrying the opponent's cuts and thrusts. The emphasis is on parries which simultaneously deflect the incoming attack and strike the opponent. The name is based on the motion with which the opponent's incoming attack is deflected.

11) **Durchwechseln** (Changing Through): Techniques for evading the opponent's blade, used when the opponent attempts to parry the swordsman's attack. Also used when the opponent attempts to beat the swordsman's point aside. The name derives from the way in which the swordsman changes the direction of his attack by passing underneath his opponent's blade. This is similar to the modern fencer's disengagement.

12) **Zucken** (Pulling Around): Repetitive, side-to-side cutting in response to the opponent's attempts to parry. The name refers to motion with which the sword is pulled or swung around the swordsman's head while striking to the other side.

13) **Durchlauffen** (Running Through): Grappling and throwing techniques used at close quarters. The technique takes its name from the way in which the swordsman ducks and "runs through" under the opponent's arms as he closes to grappling distance.

14) **Abschneiden** (Slicing Down): Drawing cuts, made with a slicing motion against one or both of the opponent's arms. Occasionally, drawing cuts were used against the opponent's face as well. These are divided into *Ober Schnitt* (made with a downwards motion) and *Unter Schnitt* (made in an upwards direction).

15) **Hende Trucken** (Pressing the Hands): Similar to *Abschneiden*, this series of techniques involves striking the opponent's hands as he attacks.

16) **Zwai Hengen** (Two Hangers): These are the primary positions formed when the blades cross. This series of techniques deals with the tactical approaches which are most useful in this situation. The name is derived from the way in which the sword blade hangs downwards toward the ground in some of the positions discussed.

17) **Acht Winden** (Eight Windings): A specialized series of attacks used when the swords are crossed. These techniques are made without ever losing contact with the opponent's blade. They allow the swordsman to retain control of the opposing sword, while simultaneously reaching around it to

deliver the attack. The name is based on the winding, turning motion of the sword along its axis.

Acknowledgements for Source Material

The comparative portions of this chapter are based on extensive correspondence and interviews with various kenjutsu instructors and practitioners. Foremost among these were Kim Taylor, Karl Friday, and Ellis Amdur. I remain indebted to a host of others, far too numerous to mention by name.

Footnotes

[1] No biographical data exists for Johannes Liechtenauer. The sole source of information concerning his life are the manuals written by the masters who followed in his footsteps. Liechtenauer was most likely born in the early or mid-14th century. Judging from clues in the text of the earliest manual, he may have been alive when it was written in 1389.

[2] For example, the writings of Master Ott appear in the manuals of Hans Talhoffer (1443) and Jud Lew (n.d.); the writings of Master Leckuechner appear in Christian Egenolph's printed work (misspelled as "Lebkommer") and Albrecht Duerer's manual (1512).

[3] A manuscript dating from 1579 at the German National Museum in Nuremberg contains a series of rhymes by members of the Marxbrueder and a rival organization, the Federfechter. Among the Marxbrueder are candlemakers, furriers, and potters; the Federfechter are goldsmiths, knifesmiths, and shoemakers. The origins of the individuals mentioned in this manuscript show how widespread the art had become by the late 16th century: Munich in Bavaria, Hof in Austria, Breslau in Silesia, Lubeck and Danzig on the Baltic coast, Dresden in Saxony. This manuscript is reproduced in the works of both Alfred Schaer (1901) and Karl Wassmansdorff (1870).

[4] Pauernfeindt, 1516.

[5] Draeger, 1973a: 70.

[6] Meyer, 1570: 2 recto.

[7] Still, as late as 1725, the Shogun Yoshimune imported the German riding instructor, Hans Jurgen Keyserling, to teach his courtiers the Western style of riding and fighting on horseback. This not only shows that some Germans made the journey east, but that they engaged in technical instruction as well. Keyserling's story appears in Hesselink (1995). Furthermore, a series of prints by the Dutch swordsman Martin Heemskerk in 1552 make clear that the German long sword style was practiced in the Netherlands. Conceivably,

Dutch swordsmen could have carried German long sword techniques with them to Japan.

8 This quote appears in the 10th century *Chanson de Geste of Girart de Roussillon.*

9 For an excellent discussion of the development of European armor, see Edge and Paddock (1988).

10 The Metropolitan Museum of Art in New York has in its collection a matched set of practice swords of a type illustrated in many of the German manuals. The statistics for these two swords follow:

Overall length: 50.6"

Blade length: 40.75"

Weight: 2 pounds, 14 ounces

11 The most widely used typology for medieval European swords is that developed by R. Ewart Oakeshott (1964). The long swords pictured in the various German manuals fall into types XIIIa, XVa, XVIa, XVII, XVIIIb, XVIIIe, and XX in Mr. Oakeshott's typology. This includes nearly all of the weapons classified variously as "war swords" or "hand-and-a-half swords."

12 Doebringer, 1389: 23 verso, 24 recto.

13 Wilhalm, 1523: 3 verso. Joerg Wilhalm produced five manuals, all of which were nearly identical.

14 See, for example, the katas depicted in Watanabe (1993). Nearly all of the attacks are downward cuts directed at the upper body and arms.

15 Ibid., Volume 1, page 12.

16 Ringeck, 1440's: 35 recto.

17 Personal communication from Dr. Karl F. Friday, who holds the rank of *shihan/menkyo kaiden* in the Kashima-Shin-ryu, a comprehensive system of battlefield martial arts which traces its origins to the 15th century.

18 See the discussion of "dynamic tension" in Amdur (1995).

19 Personal communication from Mr. Ellis Amdur, M.A. Mr. Amdur is an instructor (*shihan-dai*) in Araki-ryu Torite Kogusoku, and a master instructor (*shihan*) in Tada-ha Buko-ryu Naginatajutsu.

20 Doebringer, 1389: 19 verso.

21 Later manuals also describe a third phase, *Abziehen* (retreat), but this concept is not representative of the school as a whole.

22 Sato, 1985: 52, note 1.

23 For example, the writings of these two masters appear in the manuals of Peter von Danzig (1452) and Jud Lew (n.d.).

24 See the katas depicted in Otake (1978).

[25] See, for example, the *Great and Small Armorials of the Order of the Golden Fleece* at the Bibliotheque Nacionale and the Bibliotheque de l'Arsenal in Paris, which date from the 1430's or 1440's.

[26] Doebringer, 1389: 22 verso.

Bibliography of German Fencing Manuals

Below are listed some of the more important manuals connected with Liechtenauer's school, arranged roughly in chronological order.

Doebringer, Hanko. (1389). *Fechtbuch*. n.p. Codex Ms. 3227a at the German National Museum in Nuremberg. This is the earliest work containing the verses of Johannes Liechtenauer.

Ringeck, Sigmund. (n.d.). *Fechtbuch*. n.p. Mscr. Dresd. C 487, State Library of Saxony, Dresden, Germany. This important work dates to some time in the 1440's.

Talhoffer, Hans. (1443). *Fechtbuch*. n.p. (Gotha Codex); Ms. Chart. A 558, Research Library at Schloss Friedenstein, Gotha, Germany. This work was the first of many published by Talhoffer.

Anonymous. (n.d.). *Fechtbuch*. n.p. Codex I.6.4o.2, Central Library of the University of Augsburg. This book contains at least two 15th century works which were later bound together.

von Danzig, Peter. (1452). *Fechtbuch*. n.p. Codex 44 A 8 at the Library of the National Academy (Lincei e Corsiniana) in Rome, Italy.

Lew, Jud. (n.d.). *Fechtbuch*. n.p. Codex I.6.4o.3, Central Library of the University of Augsburg. This important work dates from around 1450-1460.

Kal, Paulus. (n.d.). *Fechtbuch*. n.p. Codex Germanicus 1507 at the State Library of Bavaria in Munich, Germany. This manual dates from around 1460-1470.

Talhoffer, Hans. (1467). *Fechtbuch*. n.p. (Munich Codex); Codex Icon. 394a at the State Library of Bavaria in Munich, Germany. This work was the last of Talhoffer's manuals.

Leckuechner, Johannes. (1482). *Fechtbuch*. n.p. Codex Germanicus 582 at the State Library of Bavaria in Munich, Germany.

von Speyer, H. (1491). *Fechtbuch*. n.p. M. I. 29, located at the Library of the University of Salzburg in Salzburg, Austria.

Falkner, Peter. (n.d.). *Fechtbuch*. n.p. Manuscript P 5012 at the Art History Museum in Vienna, Austria. A Hauptmann (captain) of the Marxbrueder, Falkner's manual appears to date from the 1490's.

Duerer, Albrecht. (1512). *Fechtbuch*. n.p. Manuscript 26-232 at the Graphics Collection at the Albertina Museum, Vienna, Austria. Albrecht Duerer was the most important artist of the Renaissance in Northern Europe. Although Duerer was not a fencing master himself, he appears to have been intimately familiar with the art.

Pauernfeindt, Andre. (1516). *Fechtbuch (Ergrundung ritterlicher kunst der fechterey)*. Vienna, Austria: n.p. This was later re-published in French under the title *La noble science des joueurs d'espee*, Antwerp, 1538.

Wilhalm, Joerg. (1522-23). *Fechtbuch*. n.p. Codex Germanicus 3711 at the State Library of Bavaria in Munich, Germany.

Wilhalm, Joerg. (1523). *Fechtbuch*. n.p. I.6.2o.2. Located at the Central Library of the University of Augsburg.

Egenolff, Christian. (1531). *Fechtbuch (Der altenn fechter an fengliche kunst . . .)*. Frankfurt am Main: n.p. This manual appeared in many editions from 1531 to 1558. Many copies of this work exist at libraries throughout Europe and the United States.

Erhart, Gregor. (1533). *Augsburg's fechtbuch*. n.p. Formerly Codex I.6.4o.4 at the Library of the University of Augsburg. Until recently thought to be lost, it was recently discovered by Professor Sydney Anglo at the Scott Collection in Glasgow, Scotland.

Mair, Paulus Hector. (n.d.). *Fechtbuch*. n.p. Mscr. Dresd. C 93/94, State Library of Saxony, Dresden, Germany. This work dates from around 1550. It is a monumental, two-volume compendium, over 1,000 pages long. Mair produced two other compendia which are nearly as long.

Anonymous. (1539). *Fechtbuch*. n.p. Probably written by a student of Hans Niedel of Salzburg; Cod. I.6.2o.5, located at the Library of the University of Augsburg in Augsburg, Germany.

Meyer, Joachim. (1570). *Grundtliche beschreibung der freyen ritterlichen und adelichen kunst des fechtens* (Basic Description of the Free, Knightly, and Noble Art of Fighting). Strasbourg (Alsace): n.p. A second edition was published in Augsburg in 1600. This important work can be found in many libraries in Europe and the United States.

Sutor, Jakob. (1612). *Fechtbuch (New kuenstliches fechtbuch)*. Frankfurt am Main: n.p. This late work devotes more space to the rapier than it does to the long sword.

Works Describing the German Fencing Manuals

Edge, David, and Paddock, John. (1988). *Arms and armor of the medieval knight.* New York: Crescent Books.

Hergsell, Gustav. (1896). *Die fechtkunst im 15 und 16 jahrhundert.* Prague: n.p.

Hils, Hans-Peter. (1985). Meister Johann Liechtenauers kunst des langen schwerts. *Europaische Hochschulschriften, Vol. 257.* Frankfurt am Main: Peter Lang.

Lochner, Karl Ernst. (1953). *Die entwicklungsphasen der europaischen fechtkunst.* Vienna: n.p.

Oakeshott, R. Ewart. (1964). *The sword and the age of chivalry.* Woodbridge, UK: Boydell Press.

Schaer, Alfred. (1901). *Die altdeutschen fechter und spielleute.* Strasbourg: n.p.

Wassmannsdorff, Alfred. (1870). *Sechs fechtschulen der Marxbrueder und Federfechter aus den jahren 1573 bis 1614.* Heidelberg: n.p.

Wierschin, Martin. (1965). *Meister Johann Liechtenauers kunst des fechtens.* Munich: Muenchener Texte und Untersuchungen zur deutschen Literatur des Mittelalters.

Works on the Japanese Sword Arts

Amdur, Ellis. (1995). Maniwa Nen-ryu. *Journal of Asian Martial Arts, 4(3),* 10-25.

Draeger, Donn F. (1973a). *Classical budo.* New York: Weatherhill.

Draeger, Donn F. (1973b). *Classical bujutsu.* New York: Weatherhill.

Harris, Victor. (1974). *A book of five rings.* Woodstock, NY: The Overlook Press.

Hesselink, Reinier H. (1995). The warrior's prayer—Tokugawa Yoshimune revives the yabusame ceremony. *The Journal of Asian Martial Arts, 4(4),* 40-49.

Otake, Ritsuke. (1978). *The deity and the sword* (Vols. 1-3). Tokyo: Minato Research and Publishing Co.

Sato, Hiroaki. (1986). *The sword and the mind.* Woodstock, NY: The Overlook Press.

Stevens, John. (1984). *The sword of no sword.* Boulder, CO: Shambhala Press.

Warner, Gordon, and Draeger, Donn F. (1982). *Japanese swordsmanship: Technique and practice.* New York: Weatherhill.

Watanabe, Tadashige. (1993). *Shinkage-ryu sword techniques* (Vols. I and II). Tokyo: Sugawara Martial Arts Institute, Inc.

7

Amateur Saya Craft: Scabbards in the Making
by Richard W. Babin, Ed.D

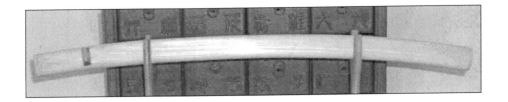

Photographs courtesy of R. Babin.

Introduction*

With care, blades may last forever, but a *saya* (scabbard) should be considered a consumable resource. Just look at the number of blades offered at auction or shows with unserviceable saya. Saya rot, dry out and split, warp, and are broken when stepped or driven upon. They chip and ding easily if dropped or struck, for example, carelessly hitting two saya together. Add to that, the saya split by the poor drawing techniques of beginning iaido or kenjutsu students and the need for a ready source of replacements is obvious. It is often hard to find a stock saya that will fit a given blade, especially without sending a blade to the source with all the inherent risk involved. Custom made saya are expensive and the wait is long, especially if it is for your favorite (or only) *iaito* (practice sword). It is also desirable to have a practice saya for each working sword so that the original saya remains pristine for display or formal purposes.

* Editor's Note: Please refer to glossary (page 158) for the meanings of Japanese terms used throughout this chapter.

The present chapter is based on the premise that building a serviceable saya is within the scope and talents of anyone moderately handy with tools. That is not to say that it is easy to produce a fine saya for an art blade. Building a high quality saya requires a fine touch with sharp instruments, extensive experience with carving, an understanding of grain, an excellent sense of proportion and, especially, a good eye for working with curves. However, it is neither difficult nor expensive to build a saya that is moderately attractive and perfectly adequate to either protect a blade or serve during drawing practice with a working blade, either a live blade or a practice blade. Furthermore, this can be done with materials that are easy to obtain and work with. While the use of power tools speeds up the process considerably, they are not critical to the end result. All that is really necessary is the patience and care to produce a good product.

The steps below represent an outline for producing a classic, undecorated saya for an inexpensive blade. They can easily be adapted to accommodate any sized blade of classical Japanese design. Pockets for accessories (*kazuka*, *kogai*), carvings or other custom features can all be added to this basic design. Figured wood may be substituted and a clear finish can be used to display the grain. Only imagination and a sense of taste limit the possibilities. It is well to keep in mind however that understatement is the hallmark of Zen influenced art.

Materials and Tools

The author's favorite domestic wood for saya is poplar. It is inexpensive, light, works cleanly, resists splitting and is easy to find. It is somewhat harder to carve than the Japanese Magnolia (*ho*) that is used for a traditional saya. The Magnolia actually works more like the basswood found in the U.S., which is a reasonable substitute for poplar, but harder to find and usually more expensive. Never use resinous wood such as pine, fir or cedar as it will eventually damage the blade.

It is convenient to work with half-inch true stock. If that cannot be purchased, thicker stock can be sawn or planed to the correct thickness. Look for pieces with a straight or gently curved, even grain, usually quarter sawn, with no knots or twists. Just like Magnolia, poplar is often a mixture of green and white wood. The color doesn't make any difference if an opaque finish is planed; otherwise white wood is desirable.

The *kurigata* (eye for attaching a belt-cord) and the caps for the *koiguchi* and *kojiri* (ends of the saya) can be made from a variety of materials. The author routinely uses domestic hedge (Osage Orange), a yellow wood that is very hard and resists splitting. Most other dense hardwoods—such as rosewood, ebony or cocobolo—will serve just as well. A traditional split resistant material to use is water buffalo horn, which can be purchased from domestic suppliers. Other possibilities include cow horn, ivory, deer antler or a plastic such as mycarta. All these materials can be formed using similar techniques. Another option is to cast them out of epoxy resin.

The best tools to use are on ones you are familiar with. Table 1 is offered only to suggest some of the options available to get the job done.

TABLE 1
A LIST OF TOOLS THAT MAY BE USED TO COMPLETE THE SAYA CONSTRUCTION

- a sheet of construction paper or cardboard
- calipers and/or ruler
- hand rip-saw and crosscut saw or table saw
- jig-saw or coping saw
- band-saw (not critical but very useful)
- table belt-sander (not critical but very useful)
- carving knife – Japanese utility knife is perfect
- 1/4" and 1/2" straight chisels
- curved gouge about 3/8" wide
- block plane of either American or Japanese design
- sanding block and garnet paper, grit sizes 60, 150, 220
- flat bastard file, 1/8" chain-saw sharpening file, small triangular file
- vise and hand drill, or drill press, 3/16" drill bit
- sandable undercoat, either aerosol or brushable
- water-proof buffing paper, 320 grit, 600 grit
- soft hair watercolor brush 3/8 to 1/2" wide
- opaque laquear or enamel, aerosol or brushable
- bottle of Heavy oil or STP® Oil Treatment
- appropriate glue depending on individual needs (epoxy, hide glue, PVA carpenter's glue)

A Japanese saya smith probably spends as much time sharpening his tools as he does slicing wood. Only a sharp tool will make a clean cut with minimal effort. Trying to cut with dull tools not only leaves a rough surface, but the extra force needed is likely to result in an eventual accident. Likewise, when using tools in general remember that when you get tired, you get dangerous—to your work and to yourself.

Layout

The basic shape of the saya is determined by the curve of the blade. A pattern can be made by tracing this curve off the blade onto a sheet of firm paper. Then trace a similar curve parallel to the first. Carry the lines out 1-2" past the length of the blade, depending on how much saya you want between the saya's closed end (*kojiri*) and the blade tip. The distance between the two lines should be twice the amount of wood you want covering the back of the blade and its edge plus the height of the blade at its widest part. Don't forget to allow enough wood at the saya's open end (*koiguchi*) to allow for the extra thickness of the metal sleeve (*habaki*) that fits between the tang and the blade. It is easiest to make these lines parallel to begin with even if you intend for the saya to taper eventually. As construction continues, the thickness of the saya's open end cap will pull the blade back out from the inside of the saya about 3/16" as it has just been marked out, but that's fine for now. The other thing to be kept in mind is that each end of the saya will need to be cut perpendicular to the tangent of the curve at that point, something that is tricky to "eyeball." This will often result in about an 1/8" of eventual shortening of the saya blank. It is not a bad plan to allow a little extra in all these initial measurements as sometimes more wood gets removed than expected or a cut must be made twice to get the direction correct. As a final step, trace the blade in the center of the paper saya, just to get a feeling for how much wood surrounds the blade. This represents your absolute margin for error and a double check that you have a pattern that leaves enough surrounding wood. Figure 1 shows what such a pattern might look like.

FIGURE I

Paper pattern in center flanked by the *wakizashi* blade and finished saya.

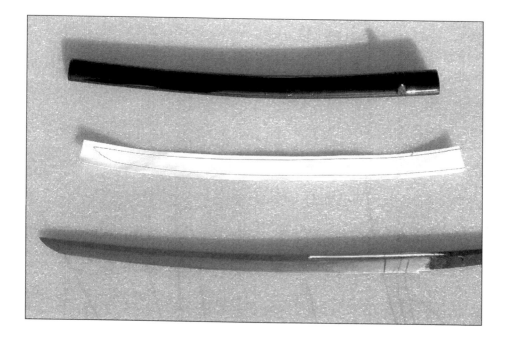

Transfer the pattern onto the surface of the wood you are using. In the process you want as much of the board's grain to run parallel to the saya as possible. A board with a gradual curve to the grain that matches the curve of the saya is ideal. More often, however, the grain will be straight. Since the open end of the saya is much more likely to be split, and requires substantially more carving than the closed end, line the grain up with the open end of the saya and allow the grain to cross diagonally across the distal end (Figure 2).

FIGURE 2

The grain of the wood runs slightly diagonally across the tip of this soon-to-be saya.

Cutting Out the Blanks

After the two blanks have been marked off on the board, they are cut out. This is most easily accomplished using a band saw. Using a wide (e.g. 1/2") blade will limit the number and degree of irregularities in the curve that you cut. A hand coping saw can also be used. Alternatively, the blanks may be cut out inside the straight lines of a rectangle using a hand or a table saw, and then the curved surfaces made using a plane or chisel (Figure 3).

FIGURE 3

The saya blank is enclosed within a rectangle. The end is being cut off square with the crosscut side of a Japanese cabinet-maker's saw. The extra (hatched) wood will be removed next with a plane or chisel.

If using the later method, remember that all plane or chisel cuts must be made in the direction of the grain (Figure 4). If cutting results in the tearing of the wood surface, turn the work around and cut from the opposite direction. Don't forget, the grain often changes direction along a piece of wood, especially one that is curved in shape.

FIGURE 4

Plane cutting in the direction with the grain will take off clean shavings. Reversing the direction of the plane will tear up the grain and/or split the wood.

Inletting the Blanks

Once the blanks approximate each other in shape, the outline of the blade is inletted into each inner surface. Be sure to clearly mark the inside/outside, as well as the *koiguchi/kojiri* (saya's ends) relationships of each blank relative to the other before beginning. All blades are not symmetric and carving the inlet into the wrong surface or in the wrong direction may result in a mismatch when the blanks are glued together.

Make sure that the open end of the blank has been cut perpendicular. Mark the blade with a magic-marker or pencil where the metal sleeve (*habaki*) ends on the tang and then remove the sleeve, placing it in a safe place. Lay the blade on the blank with the mark you just made right at the edge of the open end of the blank. Center the blade on the blank, keeping the back of the blade parallel to the convex edge of the blank. Then trace the shape of the blade onto the blank (Figure 5a).

If you're using a regular lead pencil and holding it perfectly vertical while tracing, notice that your outline will be slightly too large. Finally, using the back of the blade, draw in the approximate location of the blade's side ridge.

After this step, you will have three lines converging on the blade's tip (*mune*, *shinogi*, and *ha* lines) as it appears in Figure 2.

FIGURE 5a

The blanks have been cut out on a band saw and the blade place on top of one to check its size and, if correct, to trace the silhouette of the blade onto the blank.

FIGURES 5b-c

The gouge has made deeper cuts for the mune and *shinogi*, and a more shallow *ha*.

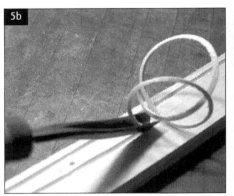

Using a "V" gouge, bead the three lines mentioned above, being mindful of the tendency of the grain to pull the gouge off the line. The line representing the sword's back and side ridges should be roughly as deep as half the thickness of the blade. The line representing the sword's sharp edge should be more shallow (Figures 5b, c). The beads are then joined by chiseling out the intervening wood with 1/4" and 1/2" chisels and the curved gouge (Figures 6a, b).

FIGURES 6a-b

The beads made with the gouge have been joined at their depth with a straight chisel and curved gouge to receive one-half the blade.

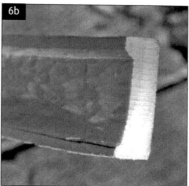

When the shape of the blade has been inletted, the size and depth can be checked by sliding the blade in and out of the half of the saya you have created. To protect the blade during these maneuvers, the author has found it useful to coat the blade with STP® Oil Treatment which will prevent finger marks, scratches and moisture from harming the blade. It also serves another purpose. When the inletting is approaching the half-silhouette of the blade, you will be able to identify the remaining high points in your carving by their shiny, oily tops. By sliding the oily blade in and out of the saya and planing off the oil left on the wood you will eventually get a good close fit. Soot or lipstick also work well for this purpose but are harder to clean up afterwards.

After one blank has been inletted to your satisfaction, transfer the measurements of your carving to the other blank. Using calipers can facilitate this. Otherwise use a ruler to transfer the line for sword's curve from one blank to the other, and then use the blade for a tracing as before.

Originally, saya were glued together using an aged rice paste. This could be easily cracked open, which allowed the inside of a saya to be cleaned from time to time and then glued back together again. In order to keep the sword's edge from opening this joint during carrying and drawing, one side of the saya was inletted deeper than exactly half the blade thickness, and the other slightly less than half. This kept the sword's edge from riding on the glue joint when the two halves were assembled. The use of modern glues often makes this process unnecessary. Another feature of some classic saya is a small hollowed out reservoir beyond the sword tip to collect blood from the replaced blade.

After inletting both blanks, they should be assembled with cord, or "C" clamps and the blade past in and out its new saya. Tight spots are identified by the oil and planed off (Figure 7). This is tiresome, but the only way to get a good fit. The blade should not rub at any point except along its back. Don't keep taking off high spots to excess, however, or the blade will rattle in the saya. Once the blade fits well, the sleeve (*habaki*) should be replaced on the tang and space for it carved into the end of each side of the saya to accommodate it (Figure 8). This must fit tightly and you must also allow for the thickness of the cap that will be placed on this end (usually 3/16" to 1/4"). Finally, if the saya is for a practice blade, the inletting may be lightly sanded. Since this might leave grit that could scratch a finely polished blade, sanding should be avoided for valuable blades.

FIGURE 7

Two halves have been joined without glue and the oily blade is being slid in and out of the inlet to identify high spots. Note the oak block used under the clamp.

FIGURE 8

The saya's open end has been carved out to accept the habaki.

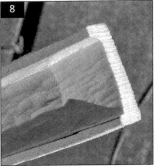

Jointing the Two Halves of the Saya

The two halves of the saya are simply glued together and clamped until the glue of choice has cured or dried. But there are some problems to consider. First, what glue should you use? If you are making a saya for a practice blade, the choice may simply be what's available. The author started out using Carpenter's glue of either the white or yellow persuasion. It cured in about two hours and was quite strong. When a saya was made for a live blade however, it was found that over time, the glue appeared to discolor the steel.

If the saya is to be opened for cleaning, hide glue—which is prepared by mixing it with and equal volume of water and heating it—works very well. It is strong and brittle, allowing the two halves of the saya to be split apart without damaging the wood. The tops of violins are actually glued on in this way, and are 'popped off' for prolonged storage of the instrument.

More recently, the author has come to use epoxy glues. These are very strong (essentially fiberglass) and, unlike other glues, can fill significant gaps in the joints, or other holes or defects in the work. They are stronger than the wood so the sword's edge can rest upon a joint that is very solid and non-reactive. Using an epoxy with a half hour set time allows some adjustment when gluing the sides together. These completely cure in about twelve hours. For gluing on the eyepiece holding the belt-cord (kurigata) and caps, or for making minor repairs or fills, epoxy that sets up in five minutes works well and is good to go in a couple of hours. With either type, you must be careful to mix equal amounts of glue and resin or it will never set up!

Another consideration in the process of creating the glue joint is the bead of glue that gets squeezed out of the joint and into the inside of the saya. This has the potential of keeping the blade from fitting all the way into the saya and depending on the glue, could damage a good blade. To some extent you control this by using the least amount of glue necessary for the job. Apply it to both sides before joining them. Some glue however is still going to run. This is where the STP comes in again. The two saya halves are joined and clamped, but before the glue can set, the blade (with the sleeve, habaki) coated with STP can be slid in and out of the saya once, pushing the glue out of the way. The blade should then be immediately wiped clean with a cloth—and a solvent, if necessary, depending on the glue used. This is probably not appropriate for a live blade, at least an expensive one. In this case, the saya maker is probably well advised to have make a wooden model of the blade ahead of time to use for this purpose.

Clamping the two halves of the saya together should be done in the proper manner. Clamps should not be applied directly to the work. They leave crush marks that damage the surface. Furthermore, if you place a clamp in the middle of an inletted side there is the risk of splitting the work, or at least creating a permanent convexity on the inside wall which will interfere with the fit. To prevent both of these problems, blocks as wide as the saya halves are slipped between the clamps and the saya. This puts the main pressure on the edges, not the center of each half (see Figure 7). Wooden furniture clamps eliminate the need to do this. The original method of holding the sides together as the glue dried was to wrap a cord up and down the two halves. This required holding the saya in each hand and the cord in your mouth, so strong solid teeth were essential to the classical saya maker. The cord tends to crush the outside edges of the two blanks, although they are the next things to be removed.

There is an alternative method of getting to this point in saya construction that, while not suitable for a live blade, works well for a practice blade and requires less skill and minimal carving. Instead of making the saya from two inletted halves, think of making a sandwich with the two outer blanks flanking a third, thinner, inner layer. This central layer is shaped the same as the other two and then thinned to the thickness of the blade. Using either a band saw or a coping saw, the silhouette of the blade is cut from its center (Figure 9). It is then glued to one of the sidepieces. When dry, any glue run is removed from the inside and size adjustments are made to the cutout silhouette with a knife and/or chisel and the open end widened for the sleeve. The second side is then glued on.

FIGURE 9

As an alternative method, a central layer of wood the thickness of the blade has the silhouette of the blade cut out and then is sandwiched between two outer blanks, which require inletting for the habaki only.

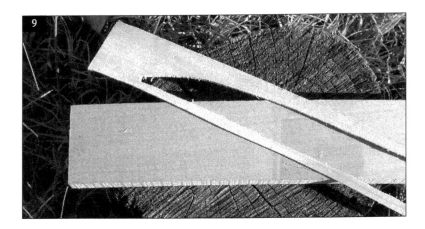

This later technique results in a saya with a rectangular central hole, not one shaped like the cross section of the blade. Therefore there is no taper to cushion the sword's edge nor "V" to receive the top of the sword's back. It is, however, perfectly adequate as a saya for an inexpensive working blade, especially if made of very soft wood. If this method is adopted, remember that the tip of many blades widen slightly at the level of the *yakote*, which separates the tip from the blade: be sure to allow enough width to the center layer to accommodate this.

Shaping the Saya

Prior to this point, it was not necessary for the two halves to be identical. Now that they are joined, they must be made to appear to be a single piece of wood. In the process, the saya must be made symmetric and the curves "faired up." Any tapering of the saya must be performed and the cross section must be rounded symmetrically. "Fairing" refers to the removal of any bumps or irregularities along a curved surface. Unlike dealing with straight lines, curves are not easily measured and must be judged and corrected primarily by using the eye. One helpful guide is the use of a uniform shaped batten sprung along the curve to help identify high areas (Figure 10a, b).

FIGURE 10a-b
Two ways of springing a batten to check the "fairness" of the curved edge of a saya.

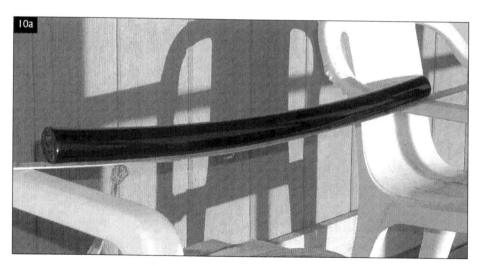

Using a plane, the upper convex surface is carefully planed at right angles to the sides. The shape of the curve is frequently checked by holding the saya at eye level and sighting along the edge of the curve. Looking at the curve going away from you will accentuate irregularities you wouldn't see otherwise and is the second trick for insuring "fairness." The high spots are then planed off, which smoothes (fairs) the curve. The concave lower surface is then cleaned up in a similar fashion. During this planing, careful attention will have to be focused on the direction of the grain. When planing the convex surface of the saya, for example, it is often necessary to cut from both ends towards the center. Since grain is in three dimensions, one side may need to be planed in an entirely different direction than the other side, depending on how you originally laid out the blanks. When this task is completed, the cross-section of the saya should be the same rectangle at all points along its length.

Once the saya is a uniform rectangle from one end to the other, the tapering can be done. While still keeping the cross-section a rectangle, use a plane to taper the saya from the open end to the closed end. Generally the height will be reduced by only a 1/16" or so, and the width by a 1/2" or less depending on the blade's length. This small amount of taper gives the saya a pleasant appearance without being obvious. It is very easy to overdo this tapering. Care must also be taken to taper in a uniform fashion, especially the sides which must maintain a flat, not curved surface. Avoid sharpening the closed end like a pencil. A belt sander is useful to cut the side taper since the surface remains flat, but it can quickly remove too much wood if used aggressively.

After establishing the proper taper, the saya is rounded using a plane. The following technique is recommend as allowing visual clues to keeping the rounding symmetric from side to side, and uniform and fair, the entire length of one side. First plane each corner off turning the cross-sectional rectangle into an octagon. Use as a guide the width of the new surface of the octagon being created, remembering that it must taper uniformly toward the closed end. Also notice the distance of the newly created corner from the midline glue joint of the top of the saya and the distance towards the center of the face. The octagon can then be inspected and evened up by eye.

Next, do the same thing one more time, taking off each of the eight corners by turning them into uniform, fair, tapering planes. Once again, even it all up by inspecting and modifying the planes. Only then, when all the newly formed shallow corners appear to be tapering evenly towards the closed end should shallow plane cuts be used to knock off these corners and turn the cross-section into a near ellipse. Take care of the tendency to remove too much from the *koiguchi* and *kojiri*, and too little from the area 2-3" back from the open end. This is more likely to occur using a western "push plane" as opposed to the use of a traditional Japanese "draw plane" (Figure 3). This is also the stage when, in an effort to correct irregularities, the width of the remaining wood can be misjudged and the center cavity entered, usually on the convex edge of the saya. (If that happens don't give up in despair, the hole can probably be filled with epoxy and never show under a paint job). Finally the saya is sanded parallel to the grain using #60 grit emery paper wrapped around a wooden block. Traditional woodworkers in Japan do not use sandpaper, but smooth their work with progressively shallower plane cuts and finish with a very mild silicon abrasive made of plant stems. Remember that even sandpaper can take off too much wood rather quickly. These steps are illustrated in Figures 11a-d.

FIGURES 11a-b-c-d

The saya undergoes a systematic transformation from square to oval and finally sanded smooth with coarse garnet paper.

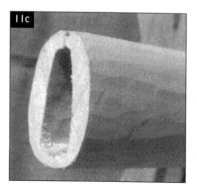
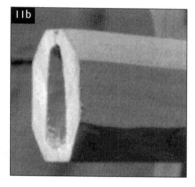

Adding End Caps

Before completely shaping the saya, the end caps for the *koiguchi* and *kojiri* should be fashioned and attached. Any hardwood, bone, antler or plastic cut into a sheet may be used. If a hardwood is utilized, make sure the grain follows the long axis of the ellipse. Place the closed end of the saya on the sheet of material close to one end and trace that end onto the sheet with a pencil. This will result in a slightly larger cap than the saya needs, but that is what you want initially. Then cut the cap out, making sure it will completely cover the end of the saya. Glue it to the *kojiri*, making sure it overlaps the sides of the saya all the way around.

Fashioning the cap for the open end requires a little more finesse. At an inch or so away from the edge of the sheet of cap material, mark the cross-sectional shape of your sleeve (*habaki*). To do this use a template cut from a piece of cardboard or an index card (Figure 12). Drill several holes inside the template for the sleeve and cut out the inside of this area with either a jigsaw or a coping saw (Figure 13a, b). Then enlarge the hole with an appropriately shaped file, remembering to slope the sides of the hole to match the taper of the sleeve. Frequent matching to the sleeve will prevent removing too much material, which would allow the sleeve to fall right through. It is generally wise to fit the cap so that there is about 1/8" of the sleeve left sticking out from the cap when placed within it. This will quickly wear in deeper with a working saya. Place the sleeve into the cap, and then place both into the saya. Then trace the saya end onto the cap blank and cut it out with a saw, keeping it if anything a little larger than necessary.

FIGURE 12

A template made from the widest part of the *habaki* (left) and a commercial buffalo horn blank (right) to be fashioned into the cap for the *koiguchi*.

FIGURE 13a-b

On the left, several holes have been drilled to facilitate cutting out the pattern as shown on the right.

Gluing the cap on requires very careful placement, since if it is off-center at all, the blade will bind when the sword is sheathed. Using the blade and the sleeve as guides during the gluing process can prevent this. Again, coat the sleeve and the blade with STP. Put the fitted cap on the sleeve loosely and then put the minimum of glue necessary on the top of the open end of the saya. Place the sword and sleeve into the saya loosely, staying away as much as possible from any glue (Figure 14). Squeeze the cap onto the surface of the saya, hold the cap firmly against the saya, and remove the blade and sleeve. If the cap slips, add some glue and try the maneuver again. Place the saya upright to dry. Immediately clean the blade and sleeve of any glue. Quick drying (about five minute) epoxy works very well for this, although water-soluble glue such as hide or carpenter's glue would be safer for a valuable blade.

Figures 14 and 15

Gluing an oversized cap of hedge on to the unfinished saya using the sleeve and blade as position guides. This cap will have to be inletted for a utility blade. Also notice the sleeve does not go all the way into the cap to allow for later fitting and wear. This open end cap of hedge is about to be filed even with the sides of the saya body, which is being protected from file damage by a piece of duct tape.

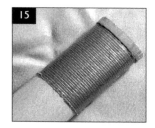

Once the glue holding the caps have dried, the caps can be filed or sanded to remove the overlap and make them flush with the outer surface of the saya. Avoid the tendency to angle the cap edge away from the saya in an attempt to protect the saya from harm. Tape can be used to protect the saya from scratches or gouges during this process (Figure 15). After the sides are parallel to the saya, the face of the caps may be shaped, for example the closed end may be slightly rounded or the open end inletted slightly (Figure 16). Once the caps are shaped to your satisfaction, the entire saya including caps should be sanded in the direction of the grain with a series of 100, 150 and 225 grit paper.

FIGURE 16

A finished end cap of deer antler sanded flush with the sides of the saya. Its corners have been rounded with a file and garnet paper.

Making and Fitting the *Kurigata*

As with the caps, the belt cord fitting (*kurigata*) can be made of any hardwood, bone, horn or plastic available. The process is essentially the same for any material and consists mostly of grinding in one guise or another. Figure 17 illustrates the sequential steps in forming a *kurigata*, in this case, out of birch. A block of the appropriate thickness is formed into a trapezoid with a saw. The base is then recessed with a file, saw or sanding wheel. Three (or more) holes are drilled through the block at the middle and the extremes of the hole through which the belt cord will pass. The sides of the trapezoid are then tapered with either a sander or a file so it is more like a pyramid. The top is then rounded and reduced in thickness. Round files used for sharpening chain saws are used to join and enlarge the central hole. Finally, files and sandpaper are used to round and smooth the entire block. Many variations of shape were used in the past, but most were kept simple and symmetric.

FIGURE 17

From 12 o'clock clockwise, a block is progressively fashioned into a *kurigata* as described in the text. The finished *kurigata* is in the center.

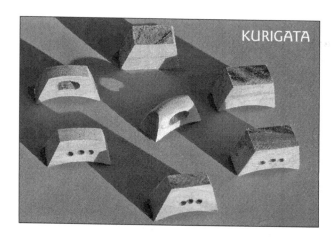

KURIGATA

Once fashioned, the *kurigata* must be attached to the *saya*. This must be after the fine sanding but before any sealer or finish is applied. The base of the *kurigata* may be filed to approximate the curve of the *saya* and glued right to its surface. Alternatively and more attractive, a groove may be cut or filed into the outerside of the saya to receive the *kurigata* (Figure 18a, b). The author prefers a combination of the above. After the *kurigata* is glued in place, the saya is ready to be finished.

FIGURE 18a-b

A groove is cut or filed into the *saya* between the lines and the *kurigata* inserted into it and glued. This *saya* has a birch kurigata and hedge caps.

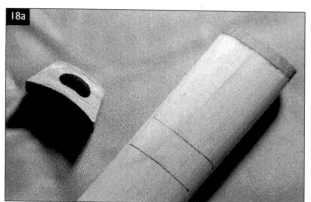

18a

18b

Finishing the Saya

However the saya is to be finished, the end result should be a smooth finish without any grain or other variations of the wood showing thorough. The most forgiving finish for a beginner is probably a clear one because the grain pattern of the wood disguises any imperfections in the finish. Several of the rub-on finishes of oil and varnish made for gunstocks work very nicely on a saya. If this option is elected, however, your glue joints and matching of caps and *kurigata* to the saya will be quite visible.

An opaque finish is far more traditional, the usual being a shinny black lacquer. There is nothing less forgiving however, than a shinny black finish. Just like on a black Porsche, every scratch and irregularity shows! Dull and textured finishes may prove to be a good compromise for the amateur saya maker as they cover poor fitting and don't emphasize surface blemishes. Also remember that some saya were wrapped with leather, cane, cord or ray skin— any of which eliminates much of the worry about the final finish.

The basis of any finish is the filling of the wood pores and other irregularities with a thick layer of undercoat. For a transparent finish, this can be done with water-soluble wood filler-sealer, or many coats of clear lacquer, enamel, or acrylic finish. Before the first coat of under coat or filler is applied, the saya should be wet with water and allowed to dry, this will raise any splinters and feathery grain. After drying, it should be lightly sanded with 225 grit paper, and then the undercoat applied. It is generally better to put many light coats of finish on over a period of time than to try to do it all with a couple of thick coats. This can be accomplished with a brush, aerosol cans or an airbrush. Sanding in between each coat with 320 grit finishing paper will result in better fill and a uniform surface. When the sanded saya shows no apparent irregularities, the external coat should be begun.

Japanese lacquer (*urushi*) is very expensive and hard to work with. It is quite toxic as it contains the active ingredient of Poison Oak. A synthetic Japanese product, under the trade name "Cashew," is available in this country and has many of the attributes of *urushi* without the toxicity. It should be thinned with turpentine. If lacquer thinner is used, there is a good chance the topcoat will cause a crackling of the previous coat thus requiring its removal. Both of these products are difficult to apply smoothly and dry very slowly. On the other hand, the quality of the surface in terms of depth and gloss is worth the work of learning to use them if your woodworking skill deserves the best finish. Good quality American lacquer can be purchased from woodworking supply stores. Use a soft fur watercolor brush to apply it and be sure to thin it sufficiently prior to application. Special brushing lacquer thinner can be found as well. Aerosol lacquer from the hardware store varies greatly in make-up and quality. If lacquer is chosen, be prepared to use 10-15 coats with wet sanding with 600 grit wet/dry sandpaper just like you'd refinish an automobile. When using lacquer, remember that one coat softens the previous one. So, if you wipe off a drip or run it will result in a crater that will have to be filled. It is better to let any drips dry thoroughly and then sand them down.

Aerosol cans of enamel intended to touch-up farm implements (John Deere Green, Ford Blue, etc.) provide hard, durable coverage while being fairly forgiving. With any aerosol or sprayer, don't get too close to the work and don't apply enough to cause a run—the curse of the spray can. If each side is alternately sprayed repeatedly, an eventual overlap on the top and the bottom of the saya will appear. Each coat should be lightly sanded before the application of the next. It is better to vary the direction from which the spray occurs or rotate the saya during the spraying process. A thin strip of cedar shingle is perfect for supporting the saya during spraying (Figures 19a, b). Also, don't forget that the spray goes all over the place, so don't spray in a close space or near anything you don't want discolored. Avoid wind and dust.

FIGURES 19a-b

Saya supported by a 1-inch strip of shingle undergoing finishing with an aerosol lacquer.

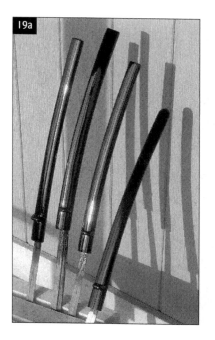

As a final encouragement to be creative, remember that whatever you initially spread on your saya, if you don't like it you can sand it off, call the residual "filler" and refinish it with something else.

References

Kapp, L., Kapp, H., and Yoshihara, Y. (1987). *The craft of the Japanese sword.* Tokyo: Kodansha International Ltd,

Young, W. (1998). *The glue book.* Newtown, CT: The Taunton Press.

GLOSSARY

Ha	The sharp edge of the sword blade
Habaki	The sleeve between tang and blade that wedges the blade into the saya
Iaito	Non-ferrous practice sword
Kashu	Type of synthetic Japanese lacquer
Kazuka	Utility blade carried in a pocket in some saya
Kissaki	The tip of the blade
Kogai	A skewer-like tool and ear cleaner stored in some saya
Koiguchi	The open end of the saya into which the sword is placed
Kojiri	The tip of the closed end of the saya
Kurigata	The fitting through which the belt cord is attached to the saya
Maharba	The widest part of the blade, usually just in front of the habaki
Mune	The top of the back of the blade, usually "V" shaped
Nakago	The tang
Sageo	The cord attaching the saya to the belt (obi)
Same	Ray-skin leather used to wrap the sword handle
Saya ate	Two saya colliding out of carelessness of the wearer(s)
Shinogi	The side ridge of a blade
Sori	The amount of curvature of a blade from habaki to kissaki
Urushi	True Japanese Lacquer – the sap of the Urushi tree
Wakizashi	Shorter companion sword of a two sword set (daisho)
Yakote	A vertical ridge separating the tip from the blade

8

A Proper Upbringing:
Kendo in Canada 1900-1950
by Joseph R. Svinth, M.A.

Akune Yuichi (left) and Tanigami Moriharu, November 1937.
Photo courtesy of Janet Matsumura Zilberman.

Kendo ("Way of the sword") appeared on British Columbia's lower mainland during the early 1910's. For instance, in 1913, Tsuzuki Kentaro established a dojo, *Yoki Kan,* at Steveston, a fishing community near the mouth of the Fraser River. In 1920, 19-year old Hayashi Rintaro became Steveston's head instructor. Seven years later, Akune Yuichi became head instructor and subsequently renamed the organization *Yosei Kan,* meaning "Proper Upbringing Hall."

By 1940, there were at least six kendo dojo in British Columbia: Vancouver, Steveston, New Westminster, Sunbury, Whonnock, and Woodfibre. Today, Steveston is part of the city of Richmond. Sunbury is south of the Fraser River's Annacis Island, Whonnock is just west of the junction of the Fraser and Stave Rivers, and Woodfibre is on the northwest side of Howe Sound, just south of Squamish.

Celebration of Matsushita Motoo's promotion to fourth-degree black-belt ranking in kendo, November 30, 1940. The venue was the Japanese Association Hall in Vancouver. *Photo reproduced by the authority of the Japanese Canadian National Museum and Archives Society, Vancouver, Canada. Photograph # 94/52.043a-c.*

Matsushita Motoo was the kendo instructor at Vancouver and Woodfibre. Although born in Vancouver around 1918, Matsushita attended high school in Japan. While in Japan he earned black-belt ranking in both judo and kendo, but preferred kendo. When he returned to Canada in the late 1930's, he immediately started a kendo club. The Vancouver classes met inside the judo school on Powell Street. "As a little girl on my way home from Japanese Language School, I remember looking in the open door to see all the action," Jean Okazaki recalled in 1999.

Akune Yuichi was the Steveston instructor. An emigrant to the US, he was small and thin, but very strong. His students were mostly of Japanese descent, and included Hayashi Masao, "Ken" Hibi Katashi, Matsumura Yeikichi, Shiomi Makami, and Tanigami Moriharu. Classes ran from October to March at the Japanese Language School. Of training at this site, judo player Doi Tomoaki told Glynn Leyshon:

> With no central heating, it was necessary to fire up the wood stove an hour before the commencement of lessons. On cold nights, the canvas covering [the floor] glittered with the frost. These were the days when wood was cut and hauled by the active members. A much-looked-for-

ward-to pleasure after an evening of practice was the hot Japanese-style bath. This four-person bath was built by Seishi Mukai and Soichi Uyeyama. The only remuneration to the instructors was tea and gas money.

The teachers at Whonnock, New Westminster, and Sunbury remain unidentified. Instruction most likely took place at the local Japanese Language Schools.

Before World War II, nearly all Canadian kendo practitioners were male. That said, in February 1940, two Seattle women demonstrated *naginatado* (a kind of halberd fencing) in Vancouver. Also in 1940, Matsushita Motoo's younger sister, Eiko, earned black-belt ranking in kendo and naginatado while attending a Tokyo high school. So there was interest, it was simply interrupted by World War II.

Equipment came directly from Japan. Steveston kendo practitioner Matsumura Yeikichi, recalled that his father had bought his armor while visiting Japan. The cost was about $100—a big sum during the Depression.

In those days, color-belt grades (*kyu*) did not receive certificates. Instead instructors simply told them what rank they held. On the other hand, black belts received certificates from Japan. Usually the instructors mailed their recommendations to the Dai Nippon Butokukai in Kyoto, but sometimes visiting instructors awarded them. Such visitors included Takano Sasaburo (a physical educator and peer of Kano Jigoro who was arguably the most influential kendo practitioner in Japan) in June 1938. Takano's son Hiromasu, a seventh-dan, also visited British Columbia during late 1939 or early 1940.

Pre-war Canadian holders of black-belt ranking were often excellent in competition. The first Canadian kendo tournament of which I am aware is the Yosei Kan tournament in Steveston held on April 18, 1931. Documentation for this event includes a photo in the Richmond City Archives. In Washington State, the first tournament of which I am aware is the Seattle Kendo Kai tournament of July 4, 1933. After that, tournaments were reasonably regular affairs in both Washington and British Columbia.

Matsumura Yeikichi, who won a Hokubei Butokukai kendo tournament held in Seattle in November 1937, recalled that travel to Seattle was via the Great Northern Railway. The Canadian team had about ten members, and in Seattle it stayed at the Holland Hotel. During the competition, Matsumura defeated nine other competitors, thus winning a prize cup awarded by Japanese Consul General Okamoto Issaku. Unfortunately, during World War II internment, the trophy was lost.

Steveston kendo tournament, April 18, 1931.
Photo courtesy of the City of Richmond Archives.

By 1940, a typical season saw a Seattle Kendo Kai tournament in November, a Hokubei Butokukai tournament in late January (venues alternated between Seattle; Tacoma; and Gresham, Oregon), and a Steveston or Vancouver tournament in mid-February.[1] If modern tournaments are any indication, then part of the competition involved each group trying to outdo the others in the quality of the food served to contestants and their parents.

"Rules regarding contests yesterday did not seem as complicated as they are today," recalled George Izui [died January 2002], then of Seattle and later Chicago:

> A contest was refereed by one person. His calls were never questioned. If a contestant had a doubt about the official's call, he tried to do better next time, so there would be no doubt. There may have been penalty rulings, but I cannot recall anyone having been charged with one. Teammates did not applaud or shout any encouragement, advice, or joyous approval. The spectators may have applauded a good contest, but I do not remember.
>
> Many of us started out to train in kendo as a sport, but later became more involved in the more difficult combination of mental and physical disciplining. There was no room for any conceited superstars. I recall our dojo having a very good kendo person [Kiyoshi Yasui] who had come home after completing his academic education in Japan. Although he was a consistent winner, he was very low-keyed and modest, and we all admired him.

Judging solely by first place victories, Steveston probably had the strongest individual kendo club in the pre-World War II Pacific Northwest. Winners received silver-plated cups donated by the Japanese consul or Dai Nippon Butokukai leaders, such as the retired general, Baron Nara Taketsugu. Recalled Tanigami Moriharu in 1999:

> [In November 1937,] Seattle had a tournament and Mr. Tokichi Nakamura of California brought two of his kendoka. They had kendo practice on the eve of the tournament. In the finals, I, a 3-dan, was challenged by a student of Mr. Nakamura for the championship and I won. For this achievement I received a trophy donated by the Japanese Consul that was presented to me by Mr. [Issaku] Okamoto.

Once the tournament was over and the trophies handed out, kendo practitioners usually celebrated by going to a restaurant for dinner. During kendo dinners, recalled Okuda Kenji, then of Seattle and now of North Vancouver, British Columbia:

> Everybody sat around a big round table, and the game was to see who could eat the most rice. These were big bowls, too, not the little bowls you sometimes see today, and the excitement started after the third bowl. If you could eat seven or eight bowls you were doing well. Some of the really big kids, of course, could eat more.

As in the United States, the Canadian Government began relocating Japanese-Canadian men almost immediately following the attack on Pearl Harbor. By September 1942, even women and children had been relocated to "concentration" camps in the Kootenays or Alberta. Although the US guarded its equivalent "relocation centers" with soldiers and barbed wire, the Canadians guarded their "Inland Housing Centres" mostly with open space. Although the American camps had fences, they did include schools, electricity, and running water, amenities the Canadian camps didn't have until the summer of 1943. Nor did the Canadian Government allow Japanese-Canadian men to enlist in the Canadian military; instead they had to join the British Army. Finally, Japanese-Canadians were told that they must either relocate east of the Rockies or prepare for post-war repatriation to Japan. This caused severe disagreements within the Japanese-Canadian community: those who chose to relocate were called dogs and those who chose to repatriate were called fools.

Anyway, while most Japanese-Americans rejected kendo as a form of cultural nationalism during World War II, many Japanese-Canadians embraced it. For example, there was a kendo club at the internment camp near Angler, Ontario as early as 1943.[2]

At its peak, the Angler camp housed about 760 men. The inmates' secretary was Robert Okazaki, who noted in June 1943:

> Our physical health has always been a major concern while we've been confined. Most of us have lost weight because of the food shortage and lack of exercise, so to help correct this problem, we are doing 'radio taiso', or radio exercises early each morning. At first, the tower guards looked down curiously as our younger internees hustled us through some very demanding military drills, but eventually even they started to exercise with us! ... We also encouraged everyone to play baseball and other outdoor sports. We skated in winter, and with a few talented judo and kendo internees, we've really delved into these two sports! It's a delight to see everyone having a good time!

Members of kendo club at POW Camp 101, Angler, Ontario, August 1944.
Photo courtesy of Jean Okazaki.

The Angler kendo dojo was called Shoko Dojo, which essentially means "Mr. Matsushita's Lakeside Kendo Club." The reference was to its location, near Lake Superior, and to its head instructor, 25-year old Matsushita Motoo.

Ken Hibi, January 1939.
Photo courtesy of Ken Hibi.

Assistant instructors included 26-year old Ken Hibi, 23-year-old Furukawa Sakuzo, and 42-year old Ichikawa Haruo. Equipment consisted of about a dozen sets of kendo armor and assorted bamboo practice weapons (*shinai*) that the Canadian YMCA arranged to have shipped to Angler from storage sites in British Columbia. By March 1944, said Okazaki, this equipment was:

getting very tattered from overuse, and is in need of major repairs! Our *shinai* [bamboo swords] were broken a long time ago, so we obtained permission from the Commandant [Lt. Col. G.C. Machum] to cut wood for new ones. We went out and split some straight, White Birch, and dried it in the shade. After shaving and smoothing each *shinai*, we applied oil and wax to make them slippery-smooth. Everyone helped, and a lot of hard work was put into each *shinai*, but White Birch is heavier than bamboo and the heft slows our movements—and if you get hit on the head, you sure see a lot of stars!

Training, said Okazaki:

began with kendo fundamentals. Training the body and mind are essential, and youngsters to fifty year olds all reverently practiced over and over again. It was such an inspiring sight! Although the Recreation Hall is a bit small, we use it as a dojo and practice four days each week. With Matsushita-sensei's enthusiastic lessons, we have tackled seventeen *men-waza* [head strikes], thirteen *kote-waza* [wrist strikes], eight *do-waza* [body strikes], and ten *tsuki-waza* [thrusting techniques]. The *waza* [techniques] are very necessary kendo elements, and along with this we also study how to judge and referee matches.

Learning to judge matches was important because the Shoko Dojo held two tournaments, one in August 1944 and another in August 1945. The individual matches were not win/lose, said Okazaki:

but clean-cut waza surfaced throughout the matches. Our spectators were surprised and awe-struck as the *shiai* [competition] showed the use of *nito-ryu* (two-sword kendo) and *naginata* [a type of halberd]. The perpetual mending and patching of our worn-out *kendo-gu* [equipment] and the many hours of practice have really paid off for us!

The Angler kendo club had maybe 50-60 members. Most had never done kendo before the war, but by the time they left three years later, many were ranked first-dan. Instructor Matsushita gave his own certificates to these people since there was no access to the Japanese associations at the time.

Following his release from Angler in April 1946, Matsushita Motoo went to Moose Jaw, Saskatchewan. After a couple years there, he accepted relocation to Japan. He opened a kendo school in Gumma Prefecture, but it lost money and eventually he had to close it. Nevertheless, he stayed with kendo and by the time of his death in the early 1990's, he was ranked seventh-dan.

Ken Hibi decided not to teach kendo in his post-war home in Thunder Bay, Ontario, in large part because he couldn't afford the multiple sets of armor a class required. In 1999, Hibi was 82-years old. During the summer, he played nine holes of golf several times a week and went walking almost every morning. His most important hobby, though, was the rock garden in front of his house. It had a stone lantern and other traditional accoutrements, and elicited many compliments from visitors. "How do you do that?" people asked him, knowing that he had had cataract surgery and other ailments associated with advanced age. He replied: "Because I took up kendo, I tell myself I must watch my conduct and behavior every day. I know I don't want to spoil my name or the name of my kendo club. Because of that, people respect me. I think, I believe, that all this is due to my kendo. I got a lot of influence from my kendo."

Ken Hibi, Thunder Bay, Ontario, 1999.
Photo courtesy of Ken Hibi.

Kaslo Kendo Club, Kaslo, BC, 1944. *Photo reproduced by the authority of the Japanese Canadian National Museum and Archives Society. Photograph # 94/86.002.*

Canadian wartime kendo practice was not restricted solely to the internment camp at Angler. For example, the Japanese Canadian National Museum
and Archives Society has a 1944 photo showing members of the Kaslo Kendo
Club located in British Columbia. Meanwhile at the Buddhist church in
Raymond, Alberta, Tanigami Moriharu taught kendo to about forty students.

Tanigami returned to Steveston after the Canadian Government author-
ized Japanese-Canadian return to the coast in 1949, and he and Hayashi
Rintaro almost immediately set about reorganizing what would become the
Steveston Kendo Club. Kendo members joined with Steveston Judo Club
members to organize permanent training areas, and in 1972, Richmond, the
Steveston Community Society, and the Japanese-Canadian Community
Association jointly financed a Martial Arts Centre. Offering judo, karate,
aikido, and kendo, the Centre has played an important role in preserving
Japanese-Canadian culture into the twenty-first century.

Notes

[1] The Seattle Kendo Kai was established before 1910 and was the oldest kendo
club in Seattle. Directly associated with the Dai Nippon Butokukai in Kyoto,
its nominal head was the Japanese consul. The Hokubei Butokukai (North
American Martial Virtue Association) had its international headquarters
outside Tokyo and its US headquarters in Alvaredo (modern Union City),
California. It established a chapter at the Seattle Buddhist Church during
the winter of 1936-1937, a move that was met with considerable distrust by
members of the Seattle Kendo Kai. Therefore, these two organizations always
held separate tournaments.

[2] Although there was never anyplace officially named Angler in Ontario,
there was a railway station of that name located just north of Lake Superior.
The station was a post office in the early 1900's. During World War II, POW
Camp 101 was built nearby to house German and Italian prisoners of war.
When the Germans started tunneling out of Angler in early 1942, the
Germans and Italians were sent to more secure camps and replaced with
Japanese-Canadian dissidents, most of whom had been arrested simply for
protesting family separations.

References

Daniels, R. (1989). *Concentration camps: North America – Japanese in the United States and Canada during World War II*. Malabar, FL: Krieger Publishing Co.

Gonnami, T. Asian Library, University of British Columbia, http://www.library .ubc.ca/asian/jcrc.html

Great Northern Daily News (Seattle).

Japanese-American Courier (Seattle).

Leyshon, G. (1998). *Judoka: The history of judo in Canada*. Gloucester, Ontario: Judo Canada.

North American Times (Seattle).

Okazaki, R., Okazaki, J., and Okazaki, C. (Trans.). (1996). *The Nisei mass evacuation group and P.O.W. Camp '101' Angler, Ontario*. Scarborough, Ontario: Markham Litho, Ltd.

Stacey, D. and Stacey, S. (1994). *Salmonopolis: The Steveston story*. Madeira Park, British Columbia: Harbour Publishing.

Acknowledgments

The assistance of the following individuals is gratefully acknowledged: Tom Bolling, Bruce Campbell, David Carter, Louis Fiset, Shane Foster, Gonnami Tsuneharu, Ken K. Hibi, George Izui, Glynn Leyshon, Matsumura Yeikichi, Brian Niiya, Jean Okazaki, Okuda Kenji, Guy Power, Heather Ross, Robert W. Smith, Tagami Reiko, Tanigami
, Kim Taylor, Ken Young, and Janet Matsumura Zilberman.

Funding Sources

Funding sources for research associated with this project included the Japanese-American National Museum and the King County Landmarks and Heritage Commission.

9

Properly Gripping the Sword
in Muso Jikiden Eishin-ryu Iaido*

by Nicklaus Suino, M.A.

Suino executes the opening thrust in *Tsuredachi* (Companions) from
the advanced standing set. *All photos courtesy of Nicklaus Suino.*

*Note: *Muso* refers to Hayashizaki Jinsuke (cir. 1546-1621), the founder of this system
who had "no equal under heaven." *Jikiden* means "direct transmission. *Eishin* refers to
Hasegawa Chikaranosuke Eishin, the name of the 7th hereditary leader of the style. The
style is said to be over 450 years old and one of the oldest extant martial arts in Japan.

Introduction

Few arts present as many challenges of detail as does iaido. Each motion
is carefully choreographed in order to achieve a highly effective use of human

anatomy, efficient energy flow, and a spare, technical beauty. Iaido performed by a real expert appears simple, but every stroke of the sword is actually composed of many crucial details. There are few practitioners of the art who have the training, character, and time in practice to master all the details to the extent necessary for real mastery. Most iaido practitioners outside of Japan and, unfortunately, many in Japan, are performing much of their art with less than maximum efficiency.

Among the aspects of Eishin-ryu Iaido that are commonly performed incorrectly is the proper grip on the handle of the *iaito* (practice sword). This is called "*tenouchi*," which literally means "inside the hands." The grip is crucial because it is the final lynchpin in the transmission of power from the body, through the arms, and into the cutting edge of the sword. A correct grip also provides "feel," which increases awareness of the sword's position and helps guide the edge through the correct path in cutting. If the grip is wrong during the major cut in each form (*kirioroshi*), the cut will not reach its potential strength, the sword will wobble excessively at the end of the cut, and the student will tend to subconsciously trick the cut by allowing a softness to creep into his hands and arms just as the cut ends. In test cutting (*tameshigiri*), a poor grip will result in a failure to cut cleanly through the target.

The Downward Cut

I have written elsewhere about the major elements of a good, straight, downward cut (see Suino, 1994), so a quick review here will suffice to reacquaint the reader. At the top of the cut, the sword is held above the head with the blade descending backward at a 45-degree angle. The elbows are wide and the heels of the hands are away from the handle (*tsuka*). As the cut begins, the arms extend and the elbows begin to straighten, causing the wrists to rotate inward. About one-third of the way through the arc of the cut, the arms should be straight and the palms should be on top of the handle. During the last two-thirds of the cut, the arms are kept straight and the shoulders pulled down. The sword should travel in a large arc, coming to rest with the butt of the handle (*tsukagashira*) one fist's distance from the abdomen. All motion should end suddenly at the end of the cut. The blade should finish almost level, with the tip (*kissaki*) level with or slightly lower than the handle. Some variation in the final angle of the sword is acceptable, but it comes from the different construction of each sword—such as the angle of the tang (*nakago*) or the shape of the handle—rather than variations in the acceptable parameters of the grip.

1) In *Tatekito* (Multi-Directional Cut) from the Sword Methods Set, the swordsman's gaze must precede the thrust to the left rear corner. 2) One interpretation of the opening move of *Tatehiza's Oroshi* (Half-Seated Set-Mountain Wind) is a wrist lock against an opponent who grabs the handle of your sword. 3) In *Yukizure* (Accompaniment), the opening cut is directed to the opponent's wrist to stop him from drawing his sword.

Gripping the Sword

There are many aspects of good grip on the sword, some of which are not technically part of *tenouchi*, such as the distance between the hands, the rotation of the hands during the cut, and the position of the wrists. Other aspects of the grip are clearly part of *tenouchi*, such as the handle's position in the palms, the extended hand position on the handle, the feeling in the fingers during the cut, and the strength of the grip. Their purpose is to provide the most efficient means of directing physical power from the arms, through the hands, and into the edge of the blade. All are important and should be carefully studied and thoroughly practiced by iaido students.

Distance Between the Hands

The hands should be placed as far apart as they can be while keeping all the fingers of the left hand on the handle. While you may read about other styles of swordsmanship that encourage students to place the left hand so that one or more fingers are off the end of the handle, this is not appropriate for Eishin-ryu iaido. In fact, this author has trained with and competed against practitioners of many Japanese lineage swordsmanship styles including Muso Shinden-ryu, Hoki-ryu, Suio-ryu, Katori Shinto-ryu, Mugai-ryu, and Jigen-ryu, and has yet to meet a teacher who advises his students to grip the handle with fewer than all ten fingers. The rationale for this is obvious: more fingers on the handle will provide more strength and control for the blade. So, while there may exist styles of swordsmanship that leave one or two fingers of the left hand off the handle, you should not employ such a grip in your practice unless specifically advised to do so by your teacher. The right hand should be as close to the finger guard (*tsuba*) as it can be (keeping in mind the extended position of the hands discussed below), so that the first knuckle of the index finger touches the finger guard. The knuckle will frequently become chafed (and eventually callused) by a textured finger guard if the grip is correct.

Figure 1

Note that the hands are placed as far apart as possible on the handle, so that there is space between them.

The space between the hands provides a degree of leverage and control that is not possible if the hands are close together. This can be distinguished from the grip on a golf club or baseball bat, in which the hands are close together, or the grip on an axe, which is appropriate for chopping.

In both golf and baseball, you want the club or bat to swing freely at the moment of impact to transmit energy to the ball. With an axe, the hands start out apart, then come together at the end of the chopping motion to let the momentum of the axe head do the work. In each of these actions, the hands are close together, creating a pivot point around which the heavy end of the tool swings.

Unlike golf clubs, baseball bats, and axes, which are heaviest at the end furthest from the user, a good long sword (*katana*) or iaido sword tends to be heavier toward its handle, with a balance point closer to the user, about two-thirds of its overall length away from the tip. Instead of chopping, our goal in cutting with a long sword is to lead with the thick middle portion of the blade (*koshi*) and follow through with a slicing motion. Downward pressure through the edge and horizontal blade movement are both important.

Hand separation on the handle allows you to maintain control of the blade so that its angle remains consistent throughout the cut while the power of the body is transmitted to the whole edge of the blade. The coordination of these two components makes efficient slicing possible.

Leverage is not the primary reason for the space between the hands. Many swords being offered for sale these days have handles exceeding 10 inches in length, some as long as 14 inches. Advertisers have suggested that the long handle helps increase leverage, and therefore power in the cut. For reasons that are very technical, a proper downward cut cannot be performed with a handle that is too long. If you are considering buying a practice sword or cutting sword (*shinken*) for iaido practice, look for a handle that is approximately 9 inches long, unless your hands are exceptionally large. If your hands press together even when they are as far apart as possible on the handle, find a sword whose handle is just long enough to allow an inch of space between them.

Suino executes the lower block in the *Yaegaki*
(Eightfold Gates) form of Eishin-ryu Iaido.

Rotation of the Hands

During the first third of the cut, the hands rotate inward slightly to bring the palms over the top of the handle. This inward movement of the hands continues, to a lesser extent, through the final two-thirds of the cut. At the end of the cut, you should have a feeling of pushing down on the handle with the palms. In Figure 1, note how the heels of the hands are rotated or pressed down over the top of the handle.

Another way to think about the hand rotation is to consider it a by-product of the motion of the elbows. As the sword is raised overhead, the elbows bend and extend out to the sides. This motion pulls the heels of the hands away from the handle. As the cut begins, the elbows straighten and the arms extend so that the heels of the hands return to press inward over the top of the handle.

Many iaido students overdo the rotation. One of the standard expressions used among iaido teachers is that the hands should rotate as though "wringing water out of a towel." Students who hear this analogy sometimes make the rotation too large, bending their wrists inward at the overhead position, and employing far too much rotation during the cut. This excessive motion deprives students of edge feel and blade control.

Instead, the fingers should move very little in relation to the handle during the cut. The majority of the motion achieved by the "rotation" of the hands should occur in the heels of the hands, which, as stated above, move away from the handle in the overhead position, and back over the handle during the first third of the cut. It is critical to emphasize, however, that the palms should end up virtually on top of the handle. Many iaido instructors can determine a student's ability just by looking at the *tenouchi*. A poorly trained student will hold the sword with the palms on the side or bottom of the handle.

Position of the Wrists

The wrists should be bent upward toward the thumbs. To better understand this position, hold your right arm straight out with your hand extended forward as though you were going to shake someone's hand. Your fingers should point straight ahead with your thumb on top and your little finger on the bottom, with your wrists in a neutral position. Without changing the position of your forearm, point your fingers upwards. You will probably find that your anatomy causes your hand to stop at an angle of about forty-five degrees.

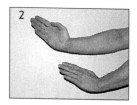 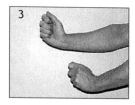

Figure 2: Hands cocked up and back. **Figure 3:** Wrist position for the downward cut.

175

Make a loose fist. Now cock the wrist back towards the knuckles. This is the approximate position for your wrists from the end of the first third of the downward cut through the end of the cut.

The purpose of this wrist position is twofold: first, along with the extended position of the hands (which is discussed below), the bent wrists help to maximize the amount of contact between the hands and the handle, thereby adding blade control; second, the position helps to ensure that the lower center portion of the palm is pressed toward the top of the handle. This removes any flex that might be caused by a loose wrist, effectively making the blade an extension of the arms.

The right hand grasps the handle of the sword from the side to begin the opening draw. This ensures that the hand is in the correct position to direct power through the blade.

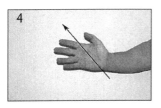
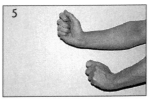

Figure 4: Line of contact for the top of the handle in the palm.
Figure 5
Figure 6: Shows an extended grip—good.

The Handle's Position in the Palms

At the end of the downward cut, the top of the handle should transcribe a line in the palms that extends from the heel of the hand, across the center of the palm, to the base of the index finger (the distal end of the first metacarpal). This provides the maximum gripping surface possible, and provides strong anatomical support for the cutting motion. In order achieve this position, the iaido student must employ the extended hand position on the handle.

The Extended Hand Position on the Handle

The grip on the handle cannot be a square grip such as one would use to grasp a dumbbell or a paddle. Instead, as discussed above, the wrists should be flexed toward the thumbs. This allows the two large fingers of each hand to open and extend slightly, adding to the overall contact between the hands and the handle, thereby adding to edge feel and blade control. Further, the wrists should also be flexed backward slightly, allowing the heels of the hands to extend forward. As noted, this helps to drive the lower center of the palm toward the top of the handle, improving the transmission of energy to the blade.

The Feeling in the Fingers During the Cut

The discussion so far has centered on the hands at the top of the handle and their role in directing power through the blade. However, the bottom of the handle is also important, because it provides feedback on the location and angle of the blade edge. The tang is the extension of the blade inside the handle. By wrapping around the handle, the inside of the practitioner's fingers provide the feedback needed to feel the angle of the edge and guide it along an accurate cutting path. For most of us, the inside of the second knuckle of each finger will line up with the bottom of the handle.

It is important for the student to cultivate sensitivity to the position of the edge. One good way to do this is to practice downward cuts while thinking of pulling the blade down with the inside of the fingers. This drill should be repeated many times. I often do this during *suburito* practice (repeated cuts with a heavy wooden sword, or *bokken*), but it requires a bokken with a very blade-like feel rather than one that is simply large and heavy. Once the feeling of guiding the blade with the inside of the fingers is established, the complete forms (*waza*) should be practiced with this same feeling in mind.

Test cutting can also be used to deepen your understanding of this aspect of *tenouchi*. Once you understand the feeling of pulling with the fingers, you should need to refresh it only occasionally by concentrating on pulling through the cuts with your fingers. If you put your mind to mastering this subtle aspect of the grip, your cuts will be stronger and much more accurate for the rest of your iaido career. Eventually, when you guide the edge properly with the inside of your fingers, it should be possible for you to cut through even very thick mats with almost no effort.

The opening cut from the *Tozume* (Blocked at the Door)
form of the *Okuiai* (secret forms) set.

The Strength of the Grip

The handle should be held with a firm, but gentle, grip. You may think of it as the neck of a goose you want to keep from escaping but don't want to strangle. The two smallest fingers of each hand should grasp most firmly, while the two larger fingers should grasp more lightly to allow the sword to "breathe." Even though the larger fingers grasp lightly, however, do not open the fingers or allow them to extend past the edge of the finger guard. Anything beyond the edge of the finger guard is at risk of being cut off during swordplay.

A proper grip guides the sword accurately and transmits the strength of the body through the edge for the entire effective portion of the cut. At the same time, too tight a grip prevents the sword from moving through its full natural arc, making cuts weak. When muscular iaido students attempt test cutting while squeezing the sword too tightly, their cuts usually fail. Only when they relax and learn to guide the sword gently through the straw mats (*tatami*) do they begin to cut smoothly and consistently. You will see that skillful practitioners move their swords on a clean, straight path, without tension, and that motions end quickly, without a lot of wobble.

Summary

During the downward cut, the hands should be placed as far apart as possible while keeping all ten fingers on the handle. The heels of the hands should rotate over the top of the handle during the cut, and the wrists should be bent upward toward the thumbs and cocked back. The top of the handle should transcribe a line from the heel of the hand, across the palm, to the base of the index finger. The hands should adopt an extended position on the handle. Iaido students should cultivate a feeling of pulling the blade edge through their cuts with the fingers. The two smaller fingers of each hand should grip firmly, and the two larger fingers should grip lightly.

In combination with the multiplicity of other movement skills required to master iaido, these checkpoints help to transmit energy from the body to the blade. By practicing each of these checkpoints with the assistance of a good teacher, students will gradually improve the strength and accuracy of their cuts. Moreover, the introspection required to analyze and apply the checkpoints will help to improve concentration and deepen understanding of the art. There is no substitute for concentrated practice over time; hopefully these guidelines will help you practice correctly and move quickly toward mastery of the wonderful, subtle art of Japanese swordsmanship.

Reference

Suino, N. (1994). How to watch iaido. *Journal of Asian Martial Arts*, 3(3): 84-91.

10

Eishin-ryu's Poetic Tradition for Transmitting Secrets of Swordsmanship

by Andrew J. Bryant, B.A.

Titles of Poems	5) Wind / Mountain Wind
1) Horizontal Clouds	6) Wave Breaking Against Rock
2) One Step of a Tiger	7) Turning Over Fish Scales
3) Lightning	8) Wave Cut
4) Floating Cloud	9) Cascading Waterfall

Within various traditional Japanese martial arts, poetry has been used to transmit oral teachings, as well as secret knowledge, or the essence of the tradition. Within the Muso Jikiden Eishin-ryu school of classical Japanese swordsmanship, there is a unique set of poems that corresponds to the intermediate level teachings (*chuden*), known as the *Tatehiza no Bu*, so called because they begin with the practitioner seated in a half kneeling position (*tatehiza*). They are said to have been created by the 7th headmaster of the tradition, Hasegawa Eishin Hidenobu (1546-1621), at some time during his headmastership in the 17th century while he was stationed at his clan's estate in Edo (Tokyo).

Passed down within the Komei Jyuku lineage these poems were written in classical Japanese. The language used is from a poetic hand and the poems' titles are similar to the names of the actual forms. They might even be the creation of Hasegawa Eishin himself; however, the actual age and author of these poems are unknown.

The poems presented here are from *Muso Jikiden Eishin-ryu, The Iai Forms and Oral Traditions of the Yamauchi Branch* (2004), by Yamakoshi Masaki and Tsukimoto Kazutake; however, all errors or inconsistencies within this chapter are the author's own. What follows is a presentation of the translated poems, along with explanations and commentaries on the corresponding techniques. The titles of the poems and techniques are listed at left.

Curiously, there is not a poem for the final technique in the Tatehiza no bu, *Makkou*. This may be due to the nature of the technique itself as a form of ordered execution (*joiuchi*).

Many members of the Muso Jikiden Eichin-ryu who are intimately familiar with the technique and paired applications have stated that the mental imagery invoked as a result of reading these poems inspired their sword technique. This is often more important than any detailed analytical discussion, and hopefully it will inspire others too.

1) Horizontal Clouds

Is it storming far away in the mountains? The cherry blossoms of Yoshino fill the hazy sky like a wisp of clouds.

Yokogumo translates as "horizontal clouds", or "cloudbank." When reading this first poem, one can imagine the cherry blossoms being so thick as to resemble such a cloud formation and mimicking those seen in the distance against a far-off mountain.

In a basic sense, the name of the technique may relate to the draw, which is a left to right horizontal cut (*yoko ichimonji*), aimed at the opponent's throat, eyes or other target of opportunity. The draw is then followed by a downward cut, ending the engagement. Yokogumo is thus very similar to the first technique of *Seiza no Bu* (*shoden*, or initial level teachings), *mae* (literally "front") or sometimes called *Shohatto* ("Initial Sword")—the quintessential iaido technique most familiar to those outside the art.

On a deeper level, one must consider the initial sentence of the poem: a question. In this case, the poem is written from the standpoint of an opponent, who is unsure of the intentions of the swordsman. One of the most important aspects of iaido (or any classical martial art) is to conceal one's true intentions from the opponent so that one may gain a significant advantage. This is the essence of this first poem and of profound importance.

181

2) One Step of a Tiger

The fierce tiger has no trouble in crossing a
thousand miles for his hind leg moves faster
forward than his fore leg to take the next step.

This second poem relates directly to aspects of the second technique of
the set, *Tora no Issoku*, or "One Step of a Tiger." This technique deals with
defending against an opponent's draw, which is blocked as the sword is
drawn—at the same time the swordsman steps back with the left foot to help
cushion the force of impact. The technical aspects of the block itself will not
be detailed here, as the wording of the poem directly describes the action of
the left leg following the block.

When one takes into consideration how four-legged animals propel
themselves forward while running, one clearly sees that while the front legs
provide support, the rear legs move forward to push off for the next propulsion.
This is how one moves forward to finish the opponent in *Tora no Issoku*.
Because a simple forward shuffle-step may not bring one within cutting
distance (*kiri-ma*), or close the combative range (*maai*) quickly enough as the
opponent retreats from his failed attack, the rear leg must be brought forward
quickly so the swordsman can adjust to any change in distance (i.e., "The
fierce tiger has no trouble in crossing a thousand miles").

In addition, it is also important to note that in this particular form,
the defending swordsman is actually countering an attack from an opponent
who is not injured (as is the case with similar forms within the school).
Therefore, one must also execute the technique quickly and with the fierceness
of a tiger.

3) Lightning

Both see the flash of lightning.
but he will not hear the crash of thunder.

The third technique of *Tatehiza no Bu* is named *Inazuma*, which translates as "lightning." In this technique, it is generally taught that the swordsman is attacked from the front with a downward cut. He defends by rising from his kneeling position and drawing the sword upward at an angle against the opponent's elbows or forearms, just before the attacking cut reaches its full extension. The swordsman then follows with a downward cut of his own as the attacker falls to the side (sliding down the sword) or otherwise stumbles back. The poem's description of the "flash of lightning" can be attributed to the sword flashing like lightning during the defender's draw.

The second portion of the poem gives insight to how quickly one should counterattack with one's own downward cut. In essence, it should be so fast that it comes between the flash of lightning and the thunder that follows, cutting down the opponent. This would typically be accomplished by remaining low during the initial draw, repositioning the sword for the decisive cut by moving the body under the sword, rather than moving the sword overhead, thus saving significant time. In doing so, the swordsman takes advantage of gravity and uses the larger leg muscles, rather than the small muscles of the hands and arms. This has obvious advantages in any technique and is not simply confined to iaido.

4) Floating Cloud

Clouds, blown forth by the wind from the foot of the
surrounding mountains, are floating over their peaks.

The fourth technique, *Ukigumo*, translates as "floating cloud." This technique can be a source of technical frustration for newer students due to its intricate footwork and circular movement. This poem describes the action of the technique perfectly; that is, the swordsman is part of the floating clouds, while the surrounding opponents are the mountain peaks.

There are many interpretations of *Ukigumo*. Some lineages teach that the application of the technique deals with applying a wrist lock (similar to aikido's *nikyo*) against an opponent who grasps the sword's handle. However, most lineages of Eishin-ryu teach that this technique deals with engaging an opponent who is two persons from the swordsman's right while sitting in formation. This opponent reaches across a bystander directly to his left (the defender's right) to grasp the defender's sword handle. Because the defender is seated in a line of fellow warriors, special movements have to be taken in order to deal with such an attack, with minimal interference from the unrelated parties that surround the attacker and defender. The manner in which the defending swordsman rises from his kneeling position and steps around the bystanders is the essence of this poem. He does so like a "floating cloud", or *Ukigumo*. The movements are intricate and require a significant degree of balance. Thus, the actual interpretation of the movements is of far less importance than what they teach: moving in balance in a confined space with a sword. To do this, one must lower his center of gravity, a trait desirable in any martial art.

5) Wind / Mountain Wind

Wind blowing swiftly down from the peak leaves no chance
for snow to pile up on the trees at the foot of the mountain.

The fifth poem deals with the technique *Oroshi* (wind), sometimes called *Yamaoroshi* (mountain wind). In this technique, the swordsman defends against an attempted grab of his sword's handle from the right. Evading the grab (or escaping from it), the defending swordsman strikes the opponent in the face with his sword handle, then draws diagonally, cutting into the opponent's neck. Next, using a pulling cut (*hikiotoshi*) braced with the left hand below the *monouchi* (first several inches of the blade), the swordsman forces the opponent down for the final decisive downward cut.

The poem has more of a cryptic feel than some of the previous examples and it is a bit more difficult to decipher. It may be tempting to interpret the poem as relating to the swift motion of the strike with the handle. However, in this case, the "wind blowing swiftly down from the peak" eloquently describes the swordsman's draw, which follows immediately after the strike. This draw of the sword is executed so quickly following the strike that it gives the opponent no time to recover from the blow, or any opportunity "for snow to pile up on the trees at the foot of the mountain."

Regardless of how one may interpret the poem, we are reminded that timing is the key to achieving victory. Just executing combative movements faster than the opponent is not always appropriate, as one may finish before the opponent and leave an opening for an adversary to exploit. Of course, the opposite may also hold true. Again, correct timing is the key.

6) Wave Breaking Against Rocks

There is no time left to steer away when the waves,
breaking on a huge rock, are about to hit the boat.

The sixth poem relates to the technique *Iwanami*, which translates as a "wave breaking against rocks." In this particular technique, the swordsman draws his blade while rising from the kneeling posture and stepping back, then turning directly left while securing the sword in the reinforced position, preparing for a thrust (*soetezuki*) against an opponent sitting beside him. The thrust is executed immediately after a stomp of the right foot, followed by the pulling cut mentioned previously (*hikiotoshi*) bringing the opponent down in preparation for the decisive final stroke.

For those familiar with *Iwanami*, the poem immediately conjures up an image of the technical movements. For those readers unfamiliar with *Iwanami*, it is essential that they understand that the poem uses a boat as a metaphor for the opponent, while the waves represent the swordsman and his sword. The sword itself moves in similar fashion to that of waves breaking against rocks on the shore. An excellent representation is the famous woodblock print by Hokusai, *Kanagawa Oki Nami Ura* ("The Great Wave Off Kanagawa"), in which an enormous wave is crashing down on a small fishing boat.

So, at this point, the poem is fairly straightforward. The opponent is the boat, while the swordsman, his sword, and the movement of the thrust are the breaking waves. What is not apparent, however, is indicated by the first part of the poem, "there is no time left to steer away." This points again to timing.

In *Iwanami*, the victorious swordsman is also the aggressor who takes advantage of the opponent's inattention to achieve victory. Here, one must have deeper knowledge of the actual technique than what lies on the surface. In *Iwanami*, the winning swordsman possibly has an accomplice sitting to the opponent's left who is talking to him, or the opponent is otherwise distracted. The swordsman quietly and slowly rises while drawing his sword low and out of the opponent's peripheral vision, then turns to face him as mentioned above. However, it is the stomp of his right foot that gets the attention of the opponent, who suddenly turns, somewhat startled, to face his attacker when "there is no time left to steer away." Such a technique takes advantage of those subtle involuntary reflexes that lie deep within our human nature. If one considers this deeply, one can think of many applications that take advantage of such instinctual reflexes.

7) Turning Over Fish Scales

Its scales withstand the heavy current,
a carp climbs upstream.

Urokogaeshi translates as "turning over fish scales," and represents the seventh technique of *Tatehiza no Bu*. This technique is similar to the first technique, *Yokogumo*, in that the swordsman executes a horizontal draw to disable an opponent, then finishes with a downward cut. In *Urokogaeshi*, however, the opponent is to the swordsman's immediate left side, seated in *tatehiza*, and the defending swordsman rises to his feet and turns to face the opponent while stepping back with his left foot during the draw.

To understand the poem, one must consider that all techniques within *Tatehiza no Bu* are at close quarters, as if in a military formation. Being right up against the opponent on his left, the swordsman must move away to gain an effective cutting distance. Because they are so close, the manner in which the swordsman turns away is similar to the scales of a carp (or any fish) against a "heavy current." The current is the opponent, while the carp is the defending swordsman. Because of the close quarters, the swordsman brushes against the opponent as he turns to draw.

In a deeper sense, we are reminded that when fighting at close quarters in general, we should move freely through the melee of opponents like a fish gliding through the water. As with our physical body, our mind must not fixate on any one opponent or action; it must move freely without hindrance.

8) Wave Cut

Rocks or ridges have to make way
when the strong waves are crashing
through the Strait of Akashi.

In this eighth poem, which corresponds to the technique called *Nami-gaeshi* (wave cut), we are given a clue in that the Akashi Strait is mentioned. The Akashi Strait is located in southern Japan, near Kobe. It separates Honshu from Awaji Island, and finally, Shikoku to the south. Shikoku, of course, is the island of the former Tosa domain, where the Eishin-ryu tradition was a closed, privately practiced tradition during feudal times (*otome ryuha*). The physical

188

characteristics of Akashi Strait would have therefore been well known to Tosa samurai traveling to and from Edo—specifically, the strong currents that exist there, as the sea is forced through the narrow strait, creating unusually large waves and turbulent surf.

To understand how the reference to waves crashing through Akashi Strait have relevance to the actual technique *Namigaeshi*, we must look at the physical movements as they relate to the application of the technique.

As stated previously, the *Tatehiza* set assumes combat at close quarters. In *Namigaeshi*, it is likely that the defending swordsman is seated in military formation with at least a row of samurai in front and behind. In this particular technique, the attack comes from the rear when an opponent rises to engage the swordsman from behind or perhaps even grabs his collar or helmet to seize the advantage.

The defending swordsman rises and turns 180 degrees counterclockwise to face the opponent. In doing so, he steps back to his original front and turns away from the line of his comrades while drawing horizontally directly over their heads. Moving away from the attacker in such a manner leaves a small opening in the rank and file where he was just seated. This opening is akin to the narrow Strait of Akashi. Like a strong wave, the swordsman then crashes through this opening in his line of comrades (i.e. the "rocks or ridges") to cut down the opponent.

9) Cascading Waterfall

Even rocks are no match against the currents of a rapid stream.

The final poem also uses water imagery to reveal the essence of the technique, which, in this case is *Takiotoshi*, or "Cascading Waterfall." *Takiotoshi* also deals with an attack from the rear. In this technique, however, an opponent grasps the swordsman's scabbard in an attempt to control the defender's movements for his own advantage prior to drawing his companion sword (*wakizashi*) or dagger (*tanto*), or possibly to assist an accomplice to the front or other direction. One may wonder, why grab the defender's scabbard at all; why not simply creep up behind and cut him down with one's sword? In this case, the attacker grasps the defender's scabbard to gain extra assurance that the opponent will have more difficulty slipping away and drawing his own sword to counterattack. Perhaps he will even gain enough of an advantage that, if the opponent does attempt to slip away, pulling up quickly on the end of the scabbard may actually dislodge his sword and send it tumbling down, out of the defender's reach.

Given the scenario of attack, the defender grasps his sword with the left hand and rises, either pushing the handle down (and the end of the scabbard up), or to the side, to force the opponent off-balance. It is essential that the defender use his body to do this, rather than his arm alone. Next, in movements similar to a "cascading waterfall," the sword is twisted and turned in a spiral, pulling it free from the opponent's grasp and further disturbing his equilibrium. The defending swordsman then quickly draws in the same motion and executes a one-handed thrust into the opponent's chest or solar plexus, followed by a decisive cut to end the encounter.

In this scenario, the opponent's grasp of the scabbard to inhibit the movements of the defender are the "rocks" referenced in the poem, and "the currents of a rapid stream" are the movements of the defender's scabbard during the technique.

The essence of the poem is that circular, often erratic movement is some-times advantageous to confuse an opponent or escape from his attack. In that sense, this strategy may even be extended further and applied to the use of timing, rather than specific physical movement. Erratic, odd timing may frustrate an opponent and disguise one's true strategy. Such manipulation of timing can be seen in other Eishin-ryu scabbard, such as "Wind Chaser" (*Oikaze*) of the initial level teaching set (*Seiza no Bu*), where it is often assumed that one is pursing the opponent from the rear. However, if one looks deeper into the movements (a clue is offered in later techniques of the school, found within the *Daikendori* paired sword set) one discovers how oddly timed running steps may be employed to confuse an opponent, seize control of combative timing and thus, it is hoped, the outcome of an engagement.

In addition to the imagery and inspiration the poems may have on those seeking to improve sword technique, they also invite deeper introspection on the layers of meaning each poem contains. Hopefully this short chapter dealing with the centuries old poetic tradition for transmitting insights for swordsman-ship will benefit today's practitioners as well.

REFERENCES

Iwata, N. (2002). *Koryu iai no hondo, Muso Jikiden Eishin Ryu*. Japan: Ski Journal Publisher.

Kamo, J. (1998). *Muso Jikiden Eishin Ryu Iaido*. Japan: Airyudo.

Suino, N. (1994, 1997). The art of Japanese swordsmanship – A manual of Eishin Ryu Iaido. New York: Weatherhill.

Yamakoshi, M., and Tsukimoto, K. (2004). *Muso Jikiden Eishin Ryu – The iai forms and oral traditions of the Yamauchi branch*. Kyoto, Japan: Maruzen Kyoto Publication Service Centre.

11

Muso Shinden-ryu Iaido
by Deborah Klens-Bigman, Ph.D.

Drawing, Cutting, and Resheathing the Japanese Sword

All styles of Japanese swordsmanship have two common characteristics: the draw, which frequently includes a cut (*nukitsuke*), and resheathing (*noto*). The draw-cut and resheathing are very basic techniques, yet even advanced students struggle to master them. My teacher, Otani Yoshiteru, often remarked that if the draw-cut was no good, the rest of the form did not matter. Japanese sword forms are based on hypothetical attack and defense situations; therefore, good drawing and cutting technique is fundamental to the "success" of the practitioner's effort against an attacker. Resheathing may be less important as a tactic, but proper technique (along with *chiburi*, shaking blood off of the sword) identifies the practitioner as a member of a specific style, and, more important, allows the sword to be resheathed safely. I will briefly note important points for proper drawing, cutting, and resheathing based on my twenty-six-year study of Muso Shinden-ryu (夢想神伝流) iaido; however, these points can be adapted to other styles of Japanese swordsmanship as well.

When I began practicing Japanese swordsmanship, Otani was frequently absent on business, so the upperclassmen made sure we got our fill of basics. At my second practice, one of them tried to instill the importance of a proper draw-cut, having me rise from a kneeling posture over and over, drawing and attempting to cut. No one told me I should have purchased knee pads for working on the very inhospitable floor. Over and over again, I rose to my knees, stepped out with my right foot, and drew the sword, a clunky, chipped loaner from the group. For the better part of an hour, the upperclassman insisted that I had to "see" my enemy in order to make an effective cut. Finally, knees aching and shoulders weary, I visualized him as my target, and made my best cut yet.

"Yes! That's what I'm talking about," he exclaimed.

Damn right, I thought.

We practiced drawing, cutting, and resheathing through long sessions of *batto-noto*—drawing with a cut; performing a short, sharp blood-flicking movement (*kochiburi*); and resheathing—on our knees. I eventually did it properly after many hours of practice.

A proper draw-cut begins with the sword grip situated at the center of the body. The draw must be silent. Any noise means the sheath is being damaged by the sword, which can cut through or split the sheath, causing potentially serious injury. The sword is drawn toward the opponent at the same time the sheath is drawn back (*sayabiki*). The right hand grip is very relaxed to begin with, and the cut itself begins just as the sword tip leaves the sheath by tightening the fingers, starting with the little finger and working across to the index finger. The resulting cut should snap out in a controlled manner, ending at the proper place (in the Muso Shinden beginning form Shohatto, the cut ends just across the opponent's face).

Proper resheathing cannot be overemphasized, as serious injury can result from improper technique. I once attended a seminar where the teacher emphasized cutting targets over any other technique. During the demonstration offered at the end of practice, his students cut well, but I was horrified at his chief student's uncertainty and lack of technique in returning the razor-sharp sword to the sheath. I wanted to leave the room, but made myself stay, thinking I might have to perform first aid to keep someone from bleeding to death! Needless to say, I lost respect for the seminar teacher in a heartbeat.

We learned proper resheathing primarily by practicing the *batto-noto* exercise noted above. From time to time an upperclassman would stand behind a newcomer, physically pulling the sheath for *sayabiki*, a technique I still use for my students.

Good resheathing technique depends on the grip of the left hand on the sheath, and pulling back the sheath. The student places the thumb at the tips of the middle and index fingers, which cover the mouth of the sheath (*koiguchi*). The student's fingers, once positioned, must never move until the end of the resheathing, when only the metal collar at the base of the blade is exposed. For resheathing in Muso Shinden-ryu's beginning set of forms, the blade is placed across the fingers of the left hand, starting at the base of the blade. The practitioner draws the blade to the right as the left hand pulls the sheath around to the back. The tip of the sword drops into the sheath. The sheath moves to meet the blade—the blade does not swing around to the mouth of the sheath. At the end of the resheathing, the grip of the sword should once again be in the center of the body, as it was at the start of the draw.

• • •

Technique 1

1a) Hand position for beginning draw with a cut (note soft grip of the right hand).

1b) Full extension of draw before the start of the cut.

1c) Full draw with a cut (for the form *Shohatto*).

1d) Full draw from the rear, showing the sheath partially pulled back.

Photography by Takashi Ikezawa.

Technique 2

2a) Left hand position for the start of resheathing. 2b) Starting position for resheathing as it is done in the beginning set of forms, at the base of the blade. 2c) Pulling the sword tip across the left hand, just prior to its insertion in the sheath. 2d) The sheath fully pulled around during resheathing, shown from the rear.

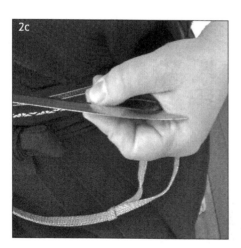

12

Niten Ichi-ryu and Shinto-ryu
by Kim Taylor, M.Sc.

The techniques discussed here come from two different schools of Japanese sword, and from two of the most important instructors for me personally and for Canadian *iaido* (a sword art) and *jodo* (use of short staff). Haruna Matsuo (1925-2002) taught the classical sword system of Niten Ichi-ryu to a few students for several years, beginning in the early 1990s.

The technique called *aisen* (合先), which I present here, came to represent the essence of Miyamoto Musashi's (c. 1584-1645) sword style for me. Direct, no-nonsense, and almost arrogant, this technique requires much confidence and not a little courage to perform. It is the final technique of a set demonstrating techniques of short sword against a long sword.

Upon learning that some of us were studying *jodo*, Haruna introduced us to Namitome Shigenori. Namitome was chair of the *jodo* section for the All Japan Kendo Federation. On a visit to Japan a few years back, we spent some time practicing in Namitome's dojo and he consented to teach us the twelve katas of Shinto-ryu sword techniques.

The technique *tsuki dachi* (突出 thrusting stance) is the final short-sword kata and final kata of the set that includes eight long-sword and four short-sword techniques. The technique has many similarities to *aisen*. Like Musashi, Muso Gonnosuke Katsuyoshi (c. 605) was not a little arrogant, as this technique seems to indicate to me. There is no trick here, no evasion. One offers a target and then takes it away. Miss the timing or the distance and you are dealing with an injury.

One memory involving *aisen* from Niten Ichi-ryu would be the amused look on Haruna's face when he demonstrated this to me for the first time: one moment I was swinging to strike through his undefended head, and the next the tip of his short sword was touching my throat, my own sword useless beside his knee and my expression obviously one of open-mouthed amazement.

The most memorable incident for *tsuki dachi* is the day I learned the technique in Namitome's dojo, with its red pine floors dented to golf-ball consistency by years of stick and sword hits. The light from the afternoon sun coming in through floor-level windows reflected from the wood in thousands of points, while a breeze through the bamboo grove behind the building made a sound I will never forget. Laughter, sweat and fear—the most delightful combination one can experience during a career in the martial arts.

Aisen and *tsuki dachi* both require the swordsman to stay directly on the attack line through the entire technique. Because of this, the opponent must be controlled by giving him a single irresistible target and the swordsman must have the patience to wait until the opponent has committed his swing toward that target. Once this happens, there is little time to react and defeat him. Fear must not be allowed to tighten muscles and delay the movements. Everything is bet on a single swing and response. There is no room for error or adjustment. They either work or they do not.

By offering your head or your hand, you must control the opponent's actions. He must believe he has no choice but to swing at the targets offered. If he thinks you will not simply run him over should he fail to attack, the technique will fail. Total commitment to the kata is required to make these techniques real.

Aisen begins by placing the short sword (*shoto*) edge down across the chest at shoulder height. This position seems completely open to attack. The swordsman walks directly toward the opponent and lets him swing. As the opponent swings at the swordsman's head, the swordsman closes his hand and extends his arm to sweep the sword off the attack line to his left side. After striking aside the sword, the swordsman rotates the *shoto* in his hand and thrusts into the throat of the opponent. In order to do this properly, the swordsman must wait until the opponent is committed to his attack, and then attack into it. In order to sweep the sword to the side, the *shoto* must sweep down the long sword's side. The most difficult skill is to adjust the pacing toward the opponent so that even if he does cut down, he will only skim the forehead of the swordsman. This lets the short sword strike the long sword at its weakest part, near the tip, where it is moving fastest. *Aisen* is a *sen no sen* timing—the swordsman attacks into the attack.

Tsuki dachi begins with the swordsman holding the *shoto*, edge to his left, directly in line with the opponent's throat and approaching boldly. If the opponent does not react, the swordsman must have the intent to thrust through the opponent's throat. Seeing this intent, the opponent will strike the *shoto* or the swordsman's right hand away before attacking on his own behalf. As the strike is made to his exposed hand, the swordsman snaps it away and then strikes down on the wrist of the opponent before he can recover. Like *aisen*, patience is demanded of this technique until the opponent commits fully to the strike. Taking the target away and striking into the opening created by the failed attack takes relaxed and unwavering movement. *Tsuki dachi* is a *go no sen*—an avoidance of the attack and a counterattack into weakness.

Technique 1: *Aisen*

1a) Hold the short sword in this position across the chest, the hand lightly open with the fingers ready to snap the blade to your left.

1b) Approach the opponent directly in a normal walking position, hips square to the front.

1c) Snap the short sword to the left, pivoting on the wrist. Do not move the right hand toward the centerline until after you have struck the sword aside. Do not move to either side of the attack line.

1d) Move the right hand to the centerline while turning the short sword so it is now edge to the right with your palm down. Move directly and strongly forward into the opponent to thrust his throat. Your feet will be together at this point.

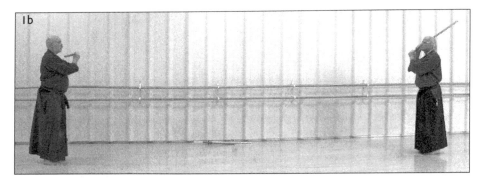

Technique 2: *Tsuki Dachi*

2a) Raise the short sword to your own throat height and hold it parallel to the ground, aimed at the opponent's throat.

2b) Approach within attack range of the opponent with the full intent of running him through.

2c) When the opponent strikes at your attacking hand, pull your right foot back to your left and at the same time swing the *shoto* up and to the side.

2d) Keeping the wrist in the same position, use your whole arm as your "sword" and strike down on the opponent's right wrist as you move your own right foot forward again into attack range.

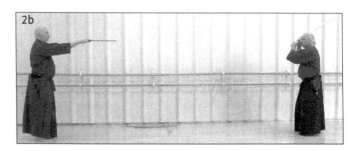

index

33128234R00115

Made in the USA
San Bernardino, CA
18 April 2019